*Foundations of Turkish Nationalism*

TO
MY WIFE

# Foundations of Turkish Nationalism

## The Life and Teachings of Ziya Gökalp

*by*

Uriel Heyd, Ph.D.

LUZAC & COMPANY LTD
AND
THE HARVILL PRESS LTD

1950

First Published 1950

Printed and bound in Great Britain by William Clowes and Sons Limited,
London and Beccles

# CONTENTS

v

# FOREWORD

Anyone who wishes to understand the spirit which informs the Constitution of the Turkish Republic and animates the minds of its statesmen will do well to read this book for two reasons. First, because Ziya Gökalp was one, and perhaps the most influential, of the spiritual founders of the Turkish Republic. Second, because the author seems very thoroughly to have penetrated the mind and grasped the philosophy of his subject—a task by no means easy, as will be seen. Furthermore, he has a first-hand acquaintance with life of modern Turkey and has studied at the University of Istanbul. He is also a master of the Turkish language—no mean accomplishment in these days, when that language is in kaleidoscopic change.

Mr. Heyd explains that Ziya Gökalp was not an original thinker, that he had no profound knowledge of European history or culture and constantly changed his views, and not infrequently adjusted his facts to suit them. But these defects do not detract from Ziya Gökalp's contribution to his country. For it has to be remembered in his defence—if, indeed, any defence be necessary—that he lived at a time when changes were rapidly taking place in Turkey and elasticity rather than rigidity of mind was the quality demanded of contemporary thinkers and statesmen. If, therefore, he was a borrower of ideas—largely from Europe— rather than a creator, and a not very logical thinker, nonetheless he had the wisdom to see in what manner Western ideas, practices and procedures could best be applied to the institutions of his own country. And let it here be noted that the most remarkable feature of the reforms of Atatürk is that while he imported the "raw material" which went to the making of many of them, yet the "goods" were made up at home to suit the taste, the traditions and manner of life of his own people. In that "making up" process

Ziya Gökalp played no small a part. But the reader will find that many of the subjects about which Ziya Gökalp wrote have more than a local or Turkish interest. The individual and the State, private versus State enterprise, the multi- and the uni-national State, and so on, are subjects of world-wide interest, and what he has to say about them is interesting. As to the value of his ideas, they are not so difficult to appraise—for they can be traced in many of the institutions of his country, in the principles embodied in the Six Arrows, and they are reflected in the present-day spirit of his people. And as all who run may read, there is much in modern Turkey that is very good, there is more which, in order to be judged, has still to stand the test of time, and all of it, as one who was an official there over thirty years ago well knows, is incomparably better than anything which existed under the old régime.

To this last sentence, I feel constrained to add these few lines. In conformity with Ziya Gökalp's views, religion and the State are to-day separated in Turkey; and some, nay most, will probably feel that the results have justified this radical step. It was no doubt the case that, in order to set their reforms in motion, the founders of the Republic felt that they were obliged to remove from the scene the forces of reaction, the most powerful of which was, in their view, religion. The individual is free to practise his religion in private, but public institutions are strictly secular. Holding the views which I do on this subject, I feel bound to ask myself what is likely to be the effect on the social and cultural life of the community of the removal of so powerful an influence on morals as was the Muslim religion while, at the same time, the door is opened to the entry for the first time of modern thought, prejudices and practices. My question must, for the time, remain unanswered, but for me it is the most important which can be asked, either of modern Turkey or of any other country.

WYNDHAM DEEDES.

# PREFACE

Many books have been written on modern Turkey, more perhaps than on any other Muslim country of the Middle East. The
progress and effect of Atatürk's drastic reforms of the political,
economic, social and cultural structure of his country have been
thoroughly investigated. Little, however, is known in the West
about the spiritual foundations of the Kemalist revolution. The
period preceding the establishment of the Turkish Republic, the
rule of the Young Turks, is still largely unexplored, especially in
its internal and ideological aspects. Yet it was during this turbulent
decade of Turkish history (1908–18) that the modern national
movement was born. Among the intellectual leaders of this movement Ziya Gökalp occupies the central place.

Although Gökalp is regarded by many as the spiritual father of
Turkish nationalism and as one of the outstanding Turkish thinkers
in modern times, his life and teachings have not yet been the
subject of any comprehensive and objective study. In Turkey
several books have been written on Gökalp, but nearly all of them
are biased and uncritical. The work of Enver Behnan Şapolyo,[1]
which contains the longest study on Gökalp in Turkish, does not
give much more than excerpts from his writings and the memoirs
of his friends. Şapolyo does not expound Gökalp's theories
systematically, nor does he express any critical opinion of his
own. Ali Nüzhet, Gökalp's son-in-law, supplies many details of
his life, but says little of his teaching. In the preface to his selections
from Gökalp's writings Hilmi Ziya Ülken has some valuable
remarks on his teachings, and it is a pity that he did not pursue
this subject further. The majority of the articles on Gökalp which
have been published in Turkish newspapers and periodicals since
his death contain only the stock eulogies along with the already

[1] See list of books and articles on Gökalp at the end of the book.

ix

well-known fundamental points of his ideas. The only attempt at a scientific treatment of the subject is the French book of the Turkish sociologist Ziyaeddin Fahri, who deals, however, mainly with Gökalp's debt to French sociology, particularly with regard to the problem of the Turkish family and its development.

European Orientalists have contributed translations and excerpts from Gökalp's writings (M. Hartmann, R. Hartmann, A. Fischer) and rather short articles on his life and work (E. Rossi, J. Deny). These scholars examined only certain parts of Gökalp's theories, and even with those they dealt mostly in a general and summary way. Moreover, their articles are based on part of Gökalp's writings only. M. Hartmann's articles as well as Muhiddin's German book on the cultural trends in modern Turkey were published when Gökalp was still in the middle of his literary activities. Rossi and Deny too were unacquainted with the many articles and poems (well over two hundred in all) which were scattered in various periodicals and had not been collected in book form.

In the present study an attempt is made to describe Gökalp's life and teachings systematically and critically within certain well-defined limits. It is concerned purely with Gökalp as the theorist of modern Turkish nationalism. For this reason and because of their doubtful scientific value, Gökalp's historical researches on the ancient Turks and their civilization are referred to only in so far as they serve as bases for his views on the problems of his time. Neither are his very numerous articles on theoretical sociology treated at any length, as in this field too Gökalp did little original thinking and merely accepted and paraphrased the theories of Western, particularly French, sociologists. It has been thought sufficient, therefore, to expound a number of the fundamental concepts underlying his sociological theories, without which his political, religious and cultural opinions cannot be fully understood. On the other hand, greater prominence is given to his views on religious problems, which the Turkish scholars, perhaps for political reasons, examined only perfunctorily. Generally, attention has been drawn to the fact that "the religious aspects of the modern Turkish . . . revolution have not yet been adequately studied."[1] Gökalp's attitude toward Islam and his ideas on its place in Turkish life are important to the understanding of both the religious development in modern Turkey and the secular trend in the Muslim world in general.

Gökalp's writings are mostly in the form of articles and poems, and even the majority of his books are only collections of writings already published in periodicals. It has been necessary, therefore, to sift all these in order to discover his ideas and weave them as far as possible into a connected system of thought. This process reveals various changes of opinion and inner contradictions in different periods of his life, and one of the chief objects of this study has been to trace Gökalp's own development as a thinker. This in turn may throw light on an interesting historical problem which up to now has not been sufficiently clarified: to what extent was Atatürk's movement the continuation of the "Committee of Union and Progress", and what is the relation between the opinions of the Young Turks and the official ideology of the present-day Turkish Republic (Kemalism). In this way Gökalp's influence on the internal structure of modern Turkey will also be fully revealed.

The sociologist as well as the student of general politics will find in Gökalp's teachings an instructive example of modern nationalist thought in an Eastern society. As recently pointed out, "a study of nationalism must follow a comparative method, . . . only the comparison of the different nationalisms all over the earth will . . . allow a just evaluation."[2] This monograph will, I hope, make a small contribution to the understanding of this major phenomenon in modern social life.

This book is based on a study, originally written in Hebrew,

[1] H. A. R. Gibb, *Modern Trends in Islam* (Chicago, 1947), pp. 46–7.
[2] H. Kohn, *The Idea of Nationalism* (New York, 1944), pp. ix–x.

which was accepted by the Hebrew University in Jerusalem as a Ph.D. thesis. As it was prepared outside Turkey, not all the material on Gökalp in Turkish was available. Of Gökalp's scattered writings all his published books and nearly all his important articles, with the exception of some of those that appeared in the *Küçük Mecmua* and other smaller periodicals, have been used. A number of Gökalp's books and most of the notes of his university lectures still exist only in manuscript. The publication of these works as well as of biographical studies by some of his friends who are still alive will shed more light on Gökalp's life and teachings.

It is my pleasant duty to acknowledge with gratitude the assistance extended to me throughout my work by Professor G. Weil of the Hebrew University, Jerusalem. Professor V. Minorsky in Cambridge and Dr. Bernard Lewis and Mr. Fahir Iz of the London School of Oriental and African Studies were kind enough to read the manuscript and offered valuable suggestions. To all of them my sincere thanks are due.

*London*.
*November*, 1947.

U. H.

# NOTE ON TRANSCRIPTION

No standard system has yet been generally accepted for the transcription of words from Oriental languages into English. In this book Turkish names and words are given in the modern Turkish spelling, which, unfortunately, is still uncertain in some cases. Most Arabic and Persian words and Islamic terms are transcribed with the help of diacritic marks, while words common in English, such as Caliph, Pasha, etc., have been rendered in their usual form. The use of these different systems of transcription makes certain inconsistencies, of course, unavoidable.

The reader who is not familiar with the modern Turkish alphabet should note the pronunciation of the following letters:

c  English *j*

ç  English *ch*

ğ  before hard vowels (a, ı, o, u) almost silent, but slightly prolonging the vowel preceding it ; before soft vowels (e, i, ö, ü)—English *y*

ı  (undotted i), something between *e* in French *le* and *u* in English *fun*

ö  French *eu* (in *jeu*)

ş  English *sh*

ü  French *u* (in *sur*)

b and d at the end of a syllable are mostly pronounced, and often spelt, *p* and *t* respectively.

The remaining Turkish letters do not present any difficulty to the English reader.

# LIST OF ABBREVIATIONS

In quoting Gökalp's writings the following abbreviations are used in the footnotes:

A.I.     Ziya Gökalp: *Altın Işık*, Istanbul, 1942.

E.       Ziya Gökalp: *Türkçülüğün Esasları*, Ankara, 1339.

G.K.     *Genç Kalemler*, Salonika, 1911.

I.M.     *İslâm Mecmuası*, Istanbul, 1914–15.

K.E.     Ziya Gökalp: *Kızıl Elma*, Istanbul, 1941.

K.M.     *Küçük Mecmua*, Diyarbekir, 1922–3.

M.T.M.   *Millî Tetebbüler Mecmuası*, I, Istanbul, 1331.

T.       Ziya Gökalp: *Türkleşmek, İslâmlaşmak, Muasırlaşmak*, Istanbul, 1918.

T.M.T.   Ziya Gökalp: *Türk Medeniyeti Tarihi*, Istanbul, 1341.

T.Y.     *Türk Yurdu*, Istanbul, 1912–14.

Y.H.     Ziya Gökalp: *Yeni Hayat*, Istanbul, 1941.

Y.M.     *Yeni Mecmua*, Istanbul, 1917–18, 1923.

Emile Durkheim's main works are quoted as follows:

L'Allemagne: "*L'Allemagne au-dessus de tout*", Paris, 1915.

Division     : *De la division du travail social* (2nd edition), Paris, 1902.

Education    : *Education et sociologie*, Paris, 1922.

Educ. morale : *L'éducation morale*, Paris, 1925.

Formes       : *Les formes élémentaires de la vie religieuse*, Paris, 1912.

Règles       : *Les règles de la méthode sociologique* (5th edition), Paris, 1910.

Sociologie   : *Sociologie et philosophie*, Paris, 1924.

Suicide      : *Le suicide*, Paris, 1897.

For details and other references see the Bibliography at the end of the book.

# PART ONE

# LIFE
# OF ZİYA GÖKALP

# LIFE OF ZİYA GÖKALP

Mehmet Ziya, better known by his pen name Ziya Gökalp,[1] was born at Diyarbekir in 1875 or 1876.[2]

Gökalp's early years coincide with a period of deep, though not lasting, changes in the Ottoman Empire. A short time after his birth, in May 1876, Sultan Abdul Aziz was deposed by the party of liberal reformers under Midhat Pasha. Abdul Aziz's successor, Murad V, showed symptoms of insanity and after reigning three months was forced to resign in favour of Abdul Hamid II. The new Sultan promised to establish a constitutional government. He appointed Midhat Pasha as Grand Vizier, and in December 1876 the new constitution was proclaimed.

The new régime did not last long. In February 1877 Midhat was dismissed, the constitution practically abolished and Parliament dissolved. During the following "period of despotism" (*devr-i istibdat*) the autocratic Sultan suppressed all political and intellectual freedom in the country by means of a large secret police and a strict censorship. The process of modernization and Westernization, which began in the days of Sultan Selim III and had been prosecuted with particular vigour since the period of Reforms (*Tanzimat*) from 1839 onwards, was interrupted for more than thirty years. A similar fate befell the Enlightenment effort of the Turkish intellectuals who from the middle of the century had followed in the wake of European and particularly French culture and proclaimed the ideals of patriotism, liberty and constitutional government. During the decades which preceded Abdul

---

[1] Unlike most European scholars, who write Gök Alp, we follow the modern Turkish usage in spelling Gökalp in *one* word. For the origin of the name, see p. 33.

[2] 1875 is the year usually accepted, but Ahmet Cemil mentions as the precise date of Gökalp's birth 27 Safar 1293, or, according to the *Rumî* calendar (Turkish Financial Year), 11 March 1292, i.e. 23 March 1876 (see *İş Mecmuası*, 39–40 (1944), pp. 20, 29).

Hamid's accession to the throne a small progressive intelligentsia had come into existence, recruited mainly from Army officers and Government officials. The Sultan rightly regarded this class as a great danger to his régime and oppressed it systematically. For support of this policy he relied on the Muslim clergy and he gained popular support by means of Pan-Islamic war-cries and demonstrations. The leaders of the reformist movement had to flee and go abroad, from where they conducted a powerful agitation against Abdul Hamid's rule. Their writings were smuggled into the Ottoman Empire and eagerly perused by the Turkish intellectuals who had been helplessly witnessing the constant decline of their country. As a result of the wars with Russia and Greece, Abdul Hamid's Empire lost large areas in the Balkans. Cyprus and Egypt were occupied by the British, and the non-Turkish communities, especially the Christians, more and more loudly demanded their independence. Owing to its desperate financial position the Ottoman State had to surrender its resources to the Western Powers which through the Capitulations and various concessions largely controlled Turkey's economic life. Save for the pessimistic and morbidly sentimental literary movement of the *Servet-i Fünun* school, the cultural life of the Turkish people had fallen into complete stagnation. No wonder that the educated class cast about for means of overthrowing Abdul Hamid and his unbearable régime.

Gökalp's native town of Diyarbekir, the administrative and cultural centre of south-eastern Anatolia, had been ruled for centuries by Arabs and Persians. Since coming under Ottoman domination in the sixteenth century, it had remained an outpost of Turkish civilization near the border of Iran and the Arab lands. In the days of Gökalp this province was largely populated by non-Turkish communities which constantly endeavoured to throw off the yoke of the Ottoman Sultan. Kurdish tribes were revolting against the Central Government, and the Armenians had, with foreign help, formed a strong underground movement which aimed at securing their complete independence. Amidst these violently conflicting national traditions and aspirations the future intellectual leader of Turkish nationalism was born. It has often been observed that "border populations are usually imbued with a particularly militant nationalism."[1] Mustafa Kemal, who led the Turkish national movement to victory, came from another border region of the Ottoman Empire, Macedonia.

Gökalp's ancestors hailed from Çermik, a small town northwest [2] of Diyarbekir. To prove his Turkish origin Gökalp himself [3] and his Turkish biographers [4] assert that Çermik, surrounded though it was by Kurdish villages, had always been inhabited by Turks. Gökalp's political opponents,[5] however, maintain that he was of Kurdish origin. Gökalp refutes this statement, but his arguments are either deductive or subjective. Without mentioning any definite family tradition on this subject he says that when he first came to Istanbul in 1896 "he felt he was a Turk". Even, he adds, if he had found out that his ancestors had come from a non-Turkish district, he would have considered himself a Turk, because education and feeling and not racial origin determine the nationality of a man. He admits that his doubts with regard to his national origin were amongst the main motives which induced him in a later period to examine the true nature of nationality.[6] In any case, Gökalp's claim to be of Turkish parentage refers to his paternal family only and does not exclude the possibility that he had Kurdish blood from his mother's side. Deny indeed thinks that his mother belonged to the well-known Kurdish family of the Pirincizade.[7]

---

[1] *Enc. of Soc. Sciences*, XI, p. 234.

[2] Both Ülken (p. 14) and Fahri (p. 4), strangely enough, describe Çermik as lying *east* of Diyarbekir.

[3] Y.M., 70, p. 54b.

[4] Ali Nüzhet, Fahri, Şapolyo.

[5] Such as Ali Kemal (see Gökalp's reply in his poem *Ali Kemal'e*, Y.H., p. 56). In an article published in the newspaper *Cumhuriyet* (22 August 1925) Yusuf Mazhar too asserts that Gökalp's ancestors were Kurds of the Zaza tribe, but this was denied by Gökalp's brother in the same paper (10 September 1925) (see Deny, pp. 3-4).

[6] Y.M., 70, p. 54 a-b; see also Y.H., p. 56; K.M., 28.      [7] Deny, pp. 2-3.

Whatever Gökalp's origin may have been, there is no doubt that he grew up in a Turkish milieu. Although he spoke Kurdish and even did some research work on this language,[1] his mother-tongue was Turkish. Gökalp's family had a distinguished record of Government service. His grandfather Mustafa Sıtkı, the son of a Mufti in the time of Mahmud II, occupied several Government posts in Van and Nusaybin, both in eastern Anatolia. His son Tevfik Efendi, Gökalp's father, was for a time director of the archives and printing press of the Diyarbekir province. Later he became editor of the Official Gazette of the *Vilâyet* and published a Government Year-Book (*salname*) of Diyarbekir. In his last years he served as head of the provincial census department. He died at an early age, leaving behind him three children and large debts.

Ziya cherished his father's memory with love and respect. He describes him as an ardent patriot who knew how to blend his religious beliefs with liberal and progressive opinions. During the short period of the first Constitution (1876-7) Tevfik published a number of articles in which he expressed his ideas openly. He instilled into his son the ideals of freedom and patriotism, the champion of which in those days was the poet Namık Kemal. His greatest wish was that Ziya should have a Western education while remaining true to Islam. Gökalp used to tell a story which is a good illustration of Tevfik's outlook. At the time when Ziya was still a schoolboy some friends of his father met at his home and suggested to Tevfik that he should send his son to Europe so that he could complete his studies there. Tevfik replied, "I am afraid that in Europe he might become a *gâvur* (unbeliever)." But when one of the guests asked, "And what will happen if he stays here?" Tevfik cried, "Then he will become an ass." [2]

After leaving the elementary school, Ziya entered the *Askerî Rüştiye* (military intermediate or lower secondary school) at

[1] He is said to have tried to form a Kurdish alphabet (Akder, p. 160).
[2] Şapolyo, p. 75.

Diyarbekir. Like most gifted Anatolian students of his generation he dreamt of going to college in Constantinople, the capital of the Empire. But while he was in one of the upper forms of the *Rüştiye* —he was fourteen or fifteen years old at the time—his father died and he had to continue his studies at the Diyarbekir secondary school (*İdadiye*).

From his early years Ziya showed a keen interest in literature. In his memoirs [1] he records that at the age of seven or eight he read with great zest the popular romances *Aşık Garip*, *Şah İsmail* and others. Later he turned his attention to plays, fiction and poetry. He read everything he could lay his hands on. His teachers did not consider him a good pupil, as he did not show much interest in the lessons taught in the old-fashioned way, which consisted in making the pupils learn text-books by heart. The only exceptions were literature, which he loved, and mathematics, which he mastered easily. His former teacher of history,[2] however, put on record that in his class too Ziya distinguished himself by his wide knowledge and independent thought.

In the secondary school Ziya began to study French, the key to Western civilization. At the same time he acquired a good Oriental education with the help of his uncle, Hasip Efendi, a Muslim scholar who settled in Diyarbekir after the death of his brother Tevfik. Hasip taught Ziya Arabic and Persian and introduced him to the works of the great Islamic philosophers, such as Ghazālī, Ibn Sīnā (Avicenna), Fārābī, Ibn Rushd and the well-known mystics Ibn 'Arabī, Jalāl ud-Dīn Rūmī and others. Ziya was particularly impressed by Ghazālī's famous autobiography *Al-munqidh min aḍ-ḍalāl*, in which the sage describes his inner struggle in his search for Truth. Ziya's excitement on reading this book may be readily understood, as his mind too was torn in those days by conflicting ideas.

---

[1] K.M., 17; 18; Y.M., 42, pp. 307b–308a.
[2] Mehmet Ali Ayni in *İş Mecmuası*, 39–40 (1944), pp. 26–7.

This was the time when the ideas of the French Revolution were inflaming the minds of Turkish youth. The headmaster of Ziya's school was a man of progressive and patriotic views who had a strong influence on his pupils. At that time there lived in Diyarbekir a group of intellectuals whom Sultan Abdul Hamid had expelled from Constantinople for their revolutionary ideas. Ziya made contact with this circle and began to read the writings of Namık Kemal, Ziya Pasha, Ahmet Midhat Efendi and other leaders of the modernist movement. Together with some friends he even ordered Turkish revolutionary literature from Europe. Ziya's connections with the underground movement became closer after the arrival in Diyarbekir of Abdullah Cevdet in the early nineties. This young Kurdish doctor, an avowed atheist and revolutionary, was imbued with the ideas of Hæckel, Büchner, Spencer and Le Bon. While studying at the Faculty of Medicine (*Tıbbiye*) in Constantinople, he took an active part in forming a secret organization which became the nucleus of the famous Committee of Union and Progress (*İttihat ve Terakki Cemiyeti*), the leaders of the 1908–9 revolution. Ziya made friends with the young doctor, although his uncle forbade him all contact with this dangerous free-thinker. It is not impossible that already at that time Abdullah Cevdet introduced him into the secret society. In any case he aroused Ziya's interest in political and social problems and perhaps turned his attention to French sociology in particular.[1]

Under the influence of these ideas Ziya wrote a number of patriotic and revolutionary poems in the years 1310–11 (1894–5). These poems, which are signed Mehmet Ziya, were not published by Gökalp himself.[2] Written in the traditional metre and in florid

---

[1] On Abdullah Cevdet's activities in Constantinople and Diyarbekir, see Şapolyo (pp. 30, 49–50, 70), and M. Hartmann (XIX, pp. 143–4). He later edited for many years the anti-clerical paper *İçtihad* which demanded full Westernization of Turkish life (*Enc. of Islām*, Suppl., pp. 55–60).

[2] Several of these poems were published by Şapolyo (pp. 35–8). See also the fragments quoted by Ali Nüzhet (p. 20).

Arabo-Persian phraseology, they called on the people to revolt against the tyrannical régime and liberate the country.

In this period of his life [1] the young Ziya experienced a shock, the impression of which was never effaced from his mind. In his memoirs which he wrote in later years,[2] he relates how in those days he passed through a typical crisis of adolescence. During his secondary school years his youthful idealism was shattered by rationalistic arguments derived mainly from his teacher of natural history, a Greek-Orthodox doctor who had some knowledge of classical and modern philosophy. In his poems written during this period [3] Ziya protests against the conception of man as an automaton—a "living machine", to use his own expression—entirely subject to the cruel laws of nature and deprived of all freedom of will and all power to do creative work and to realize his ideals. A gulf opened between the beliefs in which he had been brought up and the dictates of his reason. In his search for what he called the Supreme Truth (*Hakikat-ı kübra*) he turned to Islamic philosophy and mysticism. But in vain; they could not answer his queries. His family and friends, all devout Muslims, were dismayed at his religious doubts and accused him of heresy. Only one of them, Hacı İzzet Efendi, an educated and broad-minded man, appreciated Ziya's problems, and he used to discuss with him religious and philosophical questions for hours on end. Abdullah Cevdet's revolutionary ideas, it is true, filled Ziya with enthusiasm and made him regard freedom as an ideal worthy of every sacrifice. But under Abdul Hamid's despotic rule Ziya had no chance to fight for his ideals in a backward and reactionary town like Diyarbekir. Abdullah Cevdet's influence thus added to Ziya's inner tension without affording him an outlet for his feelings or a field for active work.

At the same time he had to face great difficulties at home. After

---

[1] Most sources give his age as seventeen, but there is reason to believe that he was one or two years older.

[2] K.M., 18.

[3] *Ibid.*

finishing school he decided to leave Diyarbekir and continue his studies in Constantinople, the centre of all political and cultural life. His family strongly objected to this plan. Hasip Efendi wanted Ziya to settle down in his native town and marry his daughter. Ziya's plea that he was still too young and desired to complete his studies received no attention. All these troubles combined filled Ziya with a sense of acute frustration and threw him into a state of despair from which he could see no escape save by committing suicide. He shot himself without, however, injuring any vital organ, and his life was saved by an operation performed by his friend Abdullah Cevdet and a Russian doctor. The bullet could not be extracted, and it remained in his skull until his death.

This event found an echo in his poem *Kızıl Elma*.[1] Turgut, the hero, attempts to shoot himself with a pistol, but is prevented at the last moment by the intervention of his beloved who shows him the way to realize his ideal. The problem of suicide always retained its importance for Gökalp. Following his teacher Durkheim who wrote a special treatise on this subject,[2] Gökalp tries in his later writings to prove that the main motive for suicide is lack of ideals and that, on the other hand, ideals are compatible with the teachings of science.[3]

Young Ziya's development is strikingly similar to that of another great Muslim modernist, the Egyptian Muhammad 'Abduh, who was born almost a generation earlier. 'Abduh too could not find satisfaction in the traditional school education and was deeply influenced by an uncle of his, Shaikh Darwīsh, who introduced him to Islamic mysticism. He also in his youth passed through a deep inner crisis. He devoted himself to ascetic exercises and looked askance at all mundane interests. As with Ziya, salvation came to him from a political leader who fought for freedom and

---

[1] K.E., pp. 32–3.          [2] *Le suicide*, Paris, 1897.
[3] K.M., 1 ; 12.   In his unpublished book on Gökalp, Ahmet Cemil maintains that Ziya was driven to suicide by the attempt of his family to force him to discontinue his friendship with a member of a hostile family. In Abdullah Cevdet's opinion Gökalp's depression was caused by a nervous disease which he had inherited from his mother (*İş Mecmuası*, 39–40 (1944), pp. 20–21).

progress, the Shaikh Jamāl ud-Dīn al-Afghānī, who—as will be shown later—indirectly influenced Gökalp too.[1]

Some time after this event Ziya's brother Nihat, who was at the time a student at the Military College of Erzincan, came to Diyarbekir to spend his vacation at home. Finding Ziya deeply depressed and full of longings for Constantinople, he promised him assistance. When he returned to college he took Ziya with him and, without telling the family, helped him to proceed to the capital.

Ziya arrived in Constantinople (1312: 1896) almost penniless. The only institution which offered him board and tuition free of charge was the Veterinary College. Having no choice, he enrolled there and attended lectures on natural science and anatomy. He devoted more time, however, to political work than to his academic studies. With the usual ceremony, moulded on the pattern of Freemasonry, he was accepted as a member of the secret society, Union and Progress, to the funds of which he contributed most of the money sent to him by his family.

During his stay in the capital Ziya met his former Christian teacher, who had also in the meantime settled in Constantinople. The doctor was in favour of the revolutionary movement. He considered, however, that the future régime should not merely imitate Western democracy but should be in harmony with the national spirit of the Turks and the social structure of the country. In his opinion it was therefore imperative as a first step to carry out a thorough investigation of the psychology and sociology of the Turkish people and to base the programme of the Turkish revolution on its results. Ziya was deeply impressed by these views and decided to provide a scientific foundation for the Turkish national movement or "Turkism", as he used to call it in later years.[2]

Gökalp himself traces the origin of his belief in Turkism to the

[1] See Osman Amin, *Muhammad 'Abduh* (Le Caire, 1944), pp. 4–7.
[2] K.M., 18.

influence of two books which he read when he was fifteen years old, Ahmet Vefik Pasha's *Lehce-i Osmanî*, a textbook of the Ottoman language, and the *Tarih-i Alem* (History of the World) by Süleyman Pasha. When he came to Constantinople the first book he got hold of was Léon Cahun's *Introduction à l'histoire de l'Asie* which, he remarks, was written "as if to encourage the ideal of Pan-Turkism."[1] At the same time he made his first contact with Hüseyinzade Ali, a young Turk from Russia, whose national and social ideas were to exercise a considerable influence on his outlook.

Ziya's revolutionary activities could not for long remain hidden from Abdul Hamid's efficient secret police. The members of the Union and Progress Society were closely watched after the attempt by some students of the Military Academy (*Harbiye*) to organize a demonstration against the Sultan in 1897. During the search of the houses of Ziya's friends in Diyarbekir illegal literature and other material was found. Among it was a letter from Ziya in which he freely expressed his political views. The police informed the authorities in Constantinople and Ziya was expelled from the Veterinary College. A short time later he was arrested and sentenced to one year's imprisonment. He spent ten months in Taşkışla, the gaol for political prisoners, and the rest of the time in two other prisons in Constantinople. In spite of his repeated requests, he was not given anything to read except the Qur'ān, which he had time to study thoroughly.

In prison Ziya met a veteran revolutionary to whose conversation he listened with great attention. In his memoirs he describes him as his third intimate teacher—Gökalp calls him *pīr*, the Persian title given to the heads of dervish orders—after his father and the Christian doctor. He regarded his advice as a "spiritual testament" and swore to follow it.[2] The old man foretold that a

---

[1] E., p. 12.

[2] It may well be that in his description of this "testament", as well as of those of his father and the Christian doctor, Gökalp uses terms and even expresses ideas which he conceived only in later years. Nevertheless, there is no reason to doubt the general truth of these memoirs.

day would come when the existing tyrannical régime would be abolished and the 1876 constitution restored. This period, however, would not last long. External pressure and internal intrigues, and above all the people's unpreparedness for a life of freedom and progress, would soon bring it to a close. The real revolution which would establish a permanent democratic order could take place only after the intellectual preparatory work had been done. The duty of the national intelligentsia was, therefore, to make use of the short period of grace afforded by the coming constitutional régime to educate the masses and prepare them for self-government. When Gökalp wrote his memoirs in 1922 [1] he could with justifiable satisfaction assert that he had fulfilled the demands of his old teacher. During the decade of the relatively liberal Young Turk rule (1908–18) he laid, in his writings, the foundations for the national and modern state which was eventually established by Mustafa Kemal, after the country had passed through a stormy transition period.

On leaving prison Ziya was exiled to Diyarbekir and confined to the town. This meant the end of his studies in Constantinople and in fact of all his university education. Gökalp never obtained an academic degree, though this did not prevent him from being later appointed professor at the Constantinople University. When he returned to his native town his uncle Hasip Efendi was already dead. Now Ziya complied with his uncle's previous request, which he had repeated in his will, and married his cousin Cevriye. Four children were born to them, a son Sedat who died at an early age and three daughters, Seniha, Hürriyet and Türkân. Seniha became the wife of the teacher Ali Nüzhet, Gökalp's biographer.

For about nine years Ziya led a peaceful and secluded life in Diyarbekir. With the exception of two Government posts in which he served for short periods he did not take up any outside work. The property his wife had inherited from her father enabled him to devote his whole time to studies. Among other subjects he

[1] K.M., 19.

began systematically to study Western and particularly French
philosophy, psychology and sociology. But he did not publish
anything during this long period, as Abdul Hamid's strict censorship prevented all expression of progressive thought.

Ziya was not so much immersed in his work as to be entirely
divorced from practical affairs. He soon became the centre of a
group of opponents of the established order. The part he played in
certain political happenings in Diyarbekir made him a prominent
figure in the province. The *Hamidiye* regiments, which were
mainly recruited from the Kurdish *Milli* tribe, had, under the
command of İbrahim Pasha, become the scourge of the province,
robbing and looting and imposing arbitrary taxes on the peasantry.
At last the Diyarbekir population decided to take the law into its
own hands, and under Ziya's leadership rose in arms against these
bands in 1906–7. Having occupied the local Post Office, they sent
a number of telegrams to the Central Government demanding its
immediate intervention. The Sultan promised to send two special
envoys to Diyarbekir to enquire into the matter and to punish the
culprits. This message appears to have been simply a device to
appease the population. Nothing was changed, and after a short
while İbrahim Pasha resumed his lawless activities. In a poem
called "The Story of İbrahim the Brigand" [1] Ziya castigated the
Government's lack of action against the Kurdish bands.

> If all of you stop half way,
> To rouse it to its duty I alone
> Shall go and call on Government . . .
> Our cry must be Justice or Death.

Eventually the Sultan was compelled to remove the *Hamidiye*
regiments and their leader İbrahim Pasha to another district. [2]

The days of Abdul Hamid's oppressive régime were now drawing to their end. In July 1908 the revolt of the Young Turks forced

---

[1] *Şakı İbrahim Paşa Destanı* (quoted in Ali Nüzhet, pp. 43–4).

[2] Some information on these events was later given by Gökalp to the corre-
spondent of the German paper *Berliner Tageblatt* (see M. Hartmann, XX,
p. 89).

the Sultan to revive the constitution and re-open Parliament. Ziya received the news with enthusiasm and supported the new order in a number of public speeches. In the remote town of Diyarbekir, however, reactionary elements, such as Government officials, religious dignitaries and heads of tribes, still retained their influence and they were able to place many obstacles in the way of those who sympathized with the Young Turk Government. Only after the abdication of the Sultan (April 1909) could Ziya and his friends work freely. Through his lectures in the local branch of Union and Progress, Ziya became known as one of its outstanding leaders in Diyarbekir. He also took part in editing the Diyarbekir papers *Peyman* and *Dicle* and published a number of articles and poems in them. In 1909 he paid a short visit to Constantinople, returning from there as inspector of the elementary schools in Diyarbekir.

A new period in Gökalp's life began in autumn 1909 when he was invited to attend the Salonika Congress of the Union and Progress movement as a representative of Diyarbekir. He was elected a member of the Central Council (*Merkez-i Umumî*), a position which he held until the dissolution of the Party after the 1918 armistice. During the Young Turk rule this body was the most important political factor behind the scenes, practically controlling all affairs of the State. Many of its members "acted much as if they were Ministers, the difference being that they were more influential than most Ministers."[1] Particularly in its second stage (from 1913 onwards) the Young Turk régime developed into a Party dictatorship, which in many respects was no less autocratic than Abdul Hamid's rule.

Settling down in Salonika, Ziya now became a national figure. The new rulers, and particularly Talât Bey, the future Grand Vizier, regarded him as a close friend. Here, at the Western fringe of the Ottoman Empire, he came into contact with liberal Turkish and European circles. A predominant rôle in the intellectual as

[1] Ahmed Emin, p. 102.

well as the economic life of Salonika was played in those days by
the non-Muslim communities, the Jews (who constituted the
majority of the population), Christians and *Dönmes*, the followers
of the Jewish pseudo-Messiah Shabbethai Zevi who had at least
outwardly embraced Islam. All these groups, which took an active
part in the Union and Progress movement, were deeply imbued
with Western and particularly French culture. Ziya's political
attitude, like that of the Young Turks in general, was strongly
influenced by the cosmopolitan and tolerant atmosphere of
Salonika. In this period he believed in the ideal of Ottomanism,
the equality of all citizens of whatever race and religion, and
consequently laid little emphasis on Islam. On the other hand, the
nationalistic tendencies and conflicts which made Salonika shortly
before the Balkan wars one of the principal danger spots of world
politics left their mark on Ziya's thought. The first signs of Turkish
nationalism can already be perceived in his writings of those years.

In this Westernized environment Ziya took a growing interest
in European philosophy and sociology. He began regularly to
lecture to a private circle on modern French thinkers, such as
Fouillée, Tarde and Le Bon. Ali Haydar, one of his friends in
this period, states [1] that he was already then studying the writings
of the French sociologist who was to become his most important
teacher, Emile Durkheim (1858–1917). Ülken, however, believes [2]
that Gökalp became interested in Durkheim only in 1912, under
the influence of his friend Hüseyinzade Ali. In any case, Durkheim's ideas do not figure conspicuously in Gökalp's works of
the Salonika period.

In 1911–12 Ziya was appointed teacher of philosophy and
sociology at the Union and Progress secondary school at Salonika.
This was, it seems, the first time that sociology was introduced
into the curriculum of any Turkish school. There can be little
doubt that this innovation was due to Ziya's initiative. In addition
he took over the direction of the Party's Youth Department. His

---

[1] Şapolyo, pp. 74–5.                    [2] Ülken, pp. 17–18.

lectures attracted large audiences and his influence, particularly on the younger generation, grew steadily. Ziya came to be regarded even by the Party leaders as one of the main intellectual forces of the movement. Yet he avoided direct participation in practical politics. He never entered any of the Cabinets formed by his party, but preferred to confine himself to theoretical research, believing that politics and academic work should be kept strictly apart.[1]

In Salonika Ziya became an active publicist. From 1911 onwards articles and poems from his pen appeared in various journals, mostly signed Tevfik Sedat, Demirtaş or Gökalp, the last of which eventually became his permanent pen-name. Gökalp, composed of the words *gök* (sky, blue) and *alp* (hero), is an old Turkish name found in the genealogical tree of the ancestors of the Ottoman Sultans.[2] In the intellectually stimulating milieu of Salonika Gökalp was encouraged, as he writes himself, to publish "the fruits of researches made during the last 17–18 years in the field of the sociology and psychology of the Turkish nation".[3]

One of the best literary journals which appeared in those days in Salonika was *Genç Kalemler* (Young Pens), edited by Ali Canip with the assistance of the popular writer Ömer Seyfettin. *Genç Kalemler* fought for the elimination from the Ottoman language of the foreign elements which were not understood by the masses of the people. The creation of a Turkish national language was regarded as a necessary condition to all cultural progress. Gökalp, who had already in 1909 published poems in the simple Turkish of the people,[4] strongly supported this endeavour. Not satisfied, however, with linguistic reform alone, he called for social reforms and for national revival in all spheres of life. Gradually Gökalp's ideal of Ottomanism was displaced by Turkish nationalism. In his

[1] See his article *Hars ve Siyaset* (Culture and Politics) in Y.M., 57.
[2] Cf. Deny, p. 6, *n.* 1.
[3] E., p. 12.
[4] E.g. the poems which he published in the Diyarbekir paper *Dicle* (quoted in Ali Nüzhet, pp. 58–60).

2

article *Yeni Hayat ve Yeni Kıymetler* (New Life and New Values) [1] the two ideals are still proclaimed side by side. But the poem *Turan*, published also in 1911 and regarded by Gökalp himself as containing the whole of his teachings in a nutshell, is an expression of undiluted Turkism.

When the Balkan war broke out in 1912, the headquarters of the Union and Progress party were moved to Constantinople and Gökalp also transferred his residence to the capital. Here his activities as writer and teacher took a new and more productive turn. With the help of Durkheim's sociology, which from now on became the main influence on his thinking, he began a systematic investigation of social and cultural problems. This most important period of Gökalp's life coincided with the last years of the Ottoman Empire. As a result of the Balkan wars the Turks lost almost all their European possessions and along with them the dream of Ottomanism vanished from the political scene. Orthodox Muslim circles, relying on the common Islamic allegiance to the Sultan-Caliph, still cherished hopes of saving the remnants of the Empire. But the revolts in Muslim provinces such as Albania (1912) and the Hijaz (1916) shattered those hopes too. No wonder that the Turkish intelligentsia became more and more attracted by the nationalist and pan-Turanian ideals which Gökalp was among the first to proclaim and to the theoretical exposition of which he now devoted all his efforts.

In Constantinople Gökalp became an active member of the *Türk Ocağı* (Turkish Hearth) club, the intellectual centre of Turkish nationalism. He was soon elected to the editorial staff of its organ, the *Türk Yurdu*, edited by his friend Akçoraoğlu Yusuf. In this journal he published inter alia his famous series of articles which later, in 1918, appeared as a separate book under the name *Türkleşmek, İslâmlaşmak, Muasırlaşmak* (Turkification, Islamization, Modernization).[2] A great number of his writings appeared in

---

[1] G.K., 8 (reprinted in Y.M., 25).
[2] Literally, "To become Turkish, Muslim, Contemporary".

other Constantinople periodicals, such as *Halka Doğru, İslâm Mecmuası,*[1] *Millî Tetebbüler Mecmuası,*[2] *İçtimaiyat Mecmuası,*[3] and particularly *Yeni Mecmua* (New Review). This important weekly started publication in 1917 with such slender means that the editors had, against Gökalp's wish, to accept subventions from the Young Turk Government. None the less it is regarded as one of the best periodicals which have ever appeared in Turkey. The most prominent writers, historians and poets of the time contributed to it regularly. Its policy was laid down by Gökalp whose influence is recognizable in most of its articles and who himself contributed to almost every one of the sixty-six issues which appeared before it ceased publication in October 1918.[4] In addition to all this Gökalp published two volumes of poetry during his Constantinople period, *Kızıl Elma* (1330: 1914-15) and *Yeni Hayat* (1918).

As a member of the Central Council of the Union and Progress party Gökalp dealt with social, legal and cultural problems. He investigated the history of the Turkish guilds, the development of the dervish orders and the question of minorities, especially of the Armenians, in Turkey. At the request of the Party leaders he prepared a report on national education [5] and took an active part in the reorganization of the libraries, the Constantinople University and the religious colleges (*medrese*). In autumn 1917 he submitted to the Party Congress a long memorandum in which he advocated the closing of these colleges and the virtual abolition of the institution of the *Şeyhülislâm*, the highest religious authority. He also called for radical reforms in the system of Pious Foundations

[1] This journal which was edited by Halim Sabit, a member of Gökalp's circle, served as the mouthpiece of the pro-nationalist liberal theology and was involved in bitter polemics with the *Sırat-ı Müstekim* and *Sebilürreşat*, the organs of orthodox Islam.

[2] Its editor was Köprülüzade Fuat, another disciple of Gökalp.

[3] This periodical too was edited by one of Gökalp's disciples, Necmettin Sadık, who was later his assistant at the University and translated a number of Durkheim's writings into Turkish.

[4] In January 1923, *Yeni Mecmua* was revived under the editorship of Falih Rıfkı and Gökalp again published a number of articles in it.

[5] Partly published in *Muallim Mecmuası*, 11-12 (1917).

(*evkaf*) and in family law. A considerable part of his suggestions were accepted by the Party and carried out by its Government during the First World War.

At the same time Gökalp strengthened his influence on the younger generation through his work as a university teacher. After having taught sociology in one of the religious colleges, he was in 1915 appointed first professor of sociology at the Constantinople University. Some of his lectures were published, the rest exist in the form of notes. Together with Yusuf Kemal, professor of economics, he founded the *İktisat Derneği* (Economic Society) where he frequently lectured on economic and social questions.

By the beginning of the First World War Gökalp had become one of the leading figures in Turkish intellectual life. Among his close friends were the Turanist Hüseyinzade Ali, the poet Yahya Kemal, the short story writer Ömer Seyfettin, the political publicist Ağaoğlu Ahmet, the historian Halim Sabit, the president of the *Türk Ocağı* Hamdullah Subhi, and many others. Some of his disciples and junior colleagues at the University were later to occupy important positions in the Turkish Republic, among them Köprülüzade Fuat, the well-known Turcologist; the novelist Halide Edib; [1] and the editors of three leading Turkish daily newspapers, Falih Rıfkı (Atay)—*Ulus*, Necmettin Sadık (Sadak) [2] —*Akşam*, and Ahmed Emin (Yalman)—*Vatan*.

The defeat of the Ottoman Empire in the First World War put an end to Gökalp's fruitful work in Constantinople. After the 1918 armistice most of the Young Turk leaders fled the country. Heedless of the warnings of his friends Gökalp stayed in the capital and continued to lecture at the University. After the Allied forces entered Constantinople he was arrested by the new Turkish Government (beginning of 1919) and detained for several months in Bekirağa Bölüğü prison. Together with other leading members of Union and Progress he was brought before a Turkish Military

---

[1] See Halide Edib, *Memoirs* (London, 1926), p. 319.
[2] Turkish Foreign Minister in 1947.

Court and accused of having taken part in the anti-Armenian agitation which had led to massacres in Anatolia during the war. According to Hakkı Süha [1] Gökalp denied that there had been any massacres, explaining that the Armenians had been killed in a war between them and the Turks whom they had stabbed in the back. He admitted, however, without hesitation that he had approved of the expulsion of Armenians. The Military Court sentenced him and his friends to be exiled from the country. In summer 1919 a British ship transferred them to Malta.

Here Gökalp established a kind of one-man university. He lectured to his fellow exiles, among whom were former Cabinet Ministers and Members of Parliament, on philosophy, sociology and literature. Despite the bitterness of exile and his own financial worries he maintained a stoical calm and helped his friends to keep up their morale. His optimism was strongly expressed in the letters he wrote from Malta to his family, mostly to his daughter Seniha. [2] In these letters as well as in his Malta lectures he continued to explain his ideal of Turkism and national revival. The defeat of the Ottoman Empire after four devastating years of war, the occupation of Turkey by its enemies, the harsh conditions of the Peace Treaty of Sèvres and the anarchy which prevailed in the country could not shatter his hope that Turkey would rise again. The first news of the Anatolian War of Liberation under Mustafa Kemal strengthened him in his belief. After the Ghazi's victory over the Greeks in 1921 Gökalp and his friends were freed and allowed to return to Turkey.

Gökalp did not find a very warm welcome. The new rulers in Ankara had little sympathy for the former Union and Progress leaders who had lost the war and ruined the country. Gökalp was not given back his position as professor at the university of Constantinople which was still under Allied occupation. Nor

---

[1] In an article published in *Türk Yurdu* and quoted in Şapolyo (p. 137).

[2] About a dozen of them have been published by his son-in-law Ali Nüzhet (pp. 101–19).

could he find a post in Ankara, the seat of Mustafa Kemal's government. He had no choice but to return with his family to his native town of Diyarbekir. For some time he taught psychology and literature at the local teachers' seminary and secondary school. At the request of the youth, who once again flocked to his house, he gave a number of public lectures. At the same time he prepared a comprehensive report on the situation of the Kurdish tribes for the Minister of Health.[1] More important were his renewed journalistic activities. With the help of friends in Ankara he managed from June 1922 onwards to publish a small weekly called *Küçük Mecmua* (Little Review) in which he strongly supported Mustafa Kemal and his policy. Owing to the lack of means, its format was very primitive. Nevertheless this modest Diyarbekir weekly, written mainly by Gökalp himself, soon acquired an honoured place in the Turkish literary world. Many of his articles were reprinted in Constantinople papers, and Falih Rifkı wrote in those days, "We have to admit that through his *Küçük Mecmua* Gökalp from Diyarbekir directs the trends of thought in Constantinople".[2] Gökalp published more than a hundred articles and poems in the *Küçük Mecmua* before it ceased publication in March 1923. Thereafter his writings were published in Constantinople papers like *Yeni Mecmua* and *Cumhuriyet*, and in *Yeni Türkiye* and *Hakimiyet-i Milliye* which appeared in Ankara.

At the end of 1922 Gökalp was appointed chairman of the official Committee for (original) Writing and Translation (*Telif ve Tercüme Heyeti*) and removed to Ankara. In his new capacity he arranged for the translation of many classical works from European languages into Turkish and himself published a book on the religion of the ancient Turks (*Türk Türesi*).

This period was one of fierce internal struggle in Turkey. After the victorious conclusion of the War of Liberation (October 1922) the former leaders of Union and Progress tried to re-establish

---

[1] Published, according to Fahri (p. 13, *n*. 3), in 1926 in a Sinop paper.
[2] Ali Nüzhet, p. 169.

their party. They invited Gökalp to join them, but he refused, preferring to remain loyal to the Ghazi. On the eve of the 1923 elections he even took an active part in the propaganda campaign of Mustafa Kemal's party, the *Anadolu ve Rumeli Müdafaa-i Hukuk Cemiyeti* (League for the Defence of the Rights of Anatolia and Rumeli), which later became the *Halk Fırkası* (People's Party). In his pamphlet *Doğru Yol* (The Right Way) he analysed and explained the programme of that party as laid down by the Ghazi in his famous Nine Basic Points (*Dokuz Umde*).[1] In the new Parliament which held its first meeting in August 1923 Gökalp represented Diyarbekir. He was also elected member of the Parliamentary Education Committee which proposed radical changes in the school curriculum and called on experts to provide a series of modern text-books. Gökalp undertook to compile several books. One of them, the first volume of the History of Turkish Civilization (*Türk Medeniyeti Tarihi*) was published in 1925, after his death. During the same period he published a collection of old Turkish stories and folktales (*Altın Işık*) and the Foundations of Turkism (*Türkçülüğün Esasları*), in which he tried to give a summary of his teachings. In Ankara Gökalp met Mustafa Kemal, but their relations never became very intimate.

For some years previous to this Gökalp's health had been steadily declining. As he could not obtain proper medical treatment in Ankara he moved to Constantinople, but the doctors of the French hospital there could not restore him to health. Several days before his death he received a telegram from Mustafa Kemal promising to defray all the expenses of a cure in Europe. In his reply Gökalp asked the Ghazi to take care of his family after his death and to publish his book on Turkish civilization. Gökalp died on 25 October 1924, at the age of forty-eight or forty-nine, and was buried at the Sultan Mahmut cemetery in Constantinople. His funeral was a national event attended by large numbers of his friends and pupils. The Turkish Parliament decided to grant a

[1] See *Oriente Mod.*, II (1922–3), pp. 707–9.

pension to his widow and daughters who had been left almost without means.

Gökalp's friends describe him as a typical scholar. Serious and taciturn, he had no taste for small talk and disliked jokes and raillery. As a rule he showed little animation and seemed to be absorbed in his own thoughts, taking little interest in his surroundings. In a discussion on subjects close to his heart, however, he would suddenly wake up, and then he knew how to express his opinions with both clarity and vigour. By nature he was most modest and exceedingly shy. His clumsy movements and lack of savoir vivre betrayed his origin, a small provincial town. To his own distress he never managed to get rid of his peculiar East-Anatolian accent. He appears to have suffered from a certain feeling of inferiority in the presence of his eloquent and vivacious friends in Constantinople who, with all their respect for his intellectual abilities and his idealism, often used to make fun of his academic outlook and his didactic manner.[1]

[1] This biography is based mainly on the following sources:

   (a) Gökalp's own writings, particularly the three articles *Felselfî vasiyetler* (K.M., 17–19);

   (b) A biography by Ali Nüzhet, Gökalp's son-in-law, valuable for his pre-Salonika period and his last years in Malta and Diyarbekir. Ali Nüzhet, although giving many interesting details, is not always reliable and he is too strongly biased in favour of Gökalp;

   (c) A study by Enver Behnan Şapolyo, Gökalp's disciple, the most comprehensive biography published hitherto. It supplements Ali Nüzhet, especially with regard to Gökalp's life in Salonika and Istanbul, and quotes important paragraphs from articles on Gökalp written by his friends, such as İbrahim Temo, Yahya Kemal, Ali Haydar, Şemsetting and others;

   (d) Shorter biographies by the Turkish writers Hilmi Ziya Ülken and Ziyaeddin Fahri and by European scholars such as Martin Hartmann, E. Rossi and J. Deny; the article *Ziyā Gök Ālp* in the *Encyclopaedia of Islām* (IV, 1231–2), also by E. Rossi;

   (e) Very short quotations from a yet unpublished Turkish book on Gökalp's life by his relative and friend Ahmet Cemil (Asena) who died in 1941 (see F. Karakoyunlu in *İş Mecmuası*, 39–40 (1944), pp. 18 *sq.*).

# PART TWO

# ZİYA GÖKALP'S
# TEACHINGS

# I

## PHILOSOPHICAL FOUNDATIONS

Except in this early years, Gökalp did not show any particular interest in philosophy. His chief preoccupation was with social and political questions and he dealt with philosophy only as far as was necessary for the theoretical foundations of his doctrines.

Gökalp explains this lack of interest in philosophy in his usual way, i.e. by the state of society in which he lived. In his opinion the time had not yet come for the Turks to occupy themselves with philosophy, which was for him purely speculative thought, devoid of any practical aim. A nation engaged in endless wars and living under difficult economic conditions could not spare any of its intellectual forces for such a luxury.[1]

The main task of the Turkish intelligentsia, he felt, should be to find ways and means of solving the burning internal and external problems of their country. The Young Turk revolution of 1908–9 affected only the political fabric of the Ottoman Empire. A second and more difficult task remained—a social revolution based on new values in all spheres of national life.[2] In his search for these values Gökalp was at the beginning attracted by the philosophy of voluntarism. His first philosophical article, which in 1911 appeared in the Salonika journal *Genç Kalemler* under the heading *The Philosophy of Today* [3] clearly shows the influence of French thinkers such as Renouvier, Boutroux and Fouillée. "The day before yesterday," writes Gökalp at the conclusion of this article, "it was regarded as the aim of philosophy to unite the sciences; philosophy was identical with general logic. Yesterday it

[1] E., pp. 172–3. In the same manner he explains the backwardness of the Turks in the spheres of science and art (K.M., 7).
[2] G.K., 8 (reprinted in Y.M., 25).
[3] G.K., 2 (quoted in Şapolyo, pp. 181–5).

43

roamed in the fields of metaphysics and took the form of general
aesthetics. Today philosophy has withdrawn into its own proper
sphere and has begun to deal with the appreciation of the political,
legal and moral values which direct our social life [1] and with the
creation of new values which may elevate humanity. The philosophy of today is general ethics . . . Its method is no more
discovery and analysis, but evaluation and creation." [2]

Here, however, as a student of natural science in the age of
positivism, Gökalp was confronted with a difficult problem. Is man
at all in a position to establish and create values? Is he not
subject to the determinism which positive science has found to
dominate the whole of existence? As Gökalp asks in one of his
earliest poems,[3] how can man, the "living machine", shake off the
shackles of the material world and rise to the realm of ideals?

In his attempt to bridge the gulf between the mechanical laws
of nature and man's freedom of creation he at first resorted to
Alfred Fouillée's doctrine of the *idées-forces* (*kuvvet-fikirler*).
The human mind conceives ideas which are capable of realizing
themselves and becoming facts as they penetrate into the external
world. But, Gökalp adds, only if these ideas fit into the general
trend of material and psychic evolution are they not mere fictions
(*mevhume*) but ideals (*mefkûre*). Just as the idées-forces direct the
course of nature by their influence on the material world, so they, and
still more their partners, the *kuvvet-hisler* (emotion-forces), in their
emergence as ideals or values, are the main factors in social life. [4]

[1] Already in this period Gökalp is interested only in *social* values.

[2] Şapolyo, p. 185. Cf. the view of the great Indian Muslim reformer
Muhammad Iqbāl for whom "its (mystical love's) highest form is the creation
of values and ideals and the endeavour to realise them" (*The Secrets of the Self*,
transl. by R. A. Nicholson (Lahore, 1944), Introduction, p. xxv).

[3] K.M., 18.

[4] G.K., 2; G.K., 8; Y.M., 27, p. 3a; 57, p. 82a. Gökalp may here be influenced
by Nietzsche whom he frequently quotes in his early writings. In German
philosophy Nietzsche is regarded as head of a philosophical school called
*Geistesphilosophie*, "die ebenfalls alle metaphysischen Weltkonstruktionen
ablehnt und die Erkenntnis auf Erfahrung einschränkt, aber . . . die Tren-
nung von Leben und Idee . . . nicht mitmacht, sondern im schöpferischen
Geistesleben den . . . Wechselbezug von Leben . . . und Ideen und Werten
. . . findet" (*Geschichte der Philosophie*, herausg. von M. Dessoir, 1925, p. 537).

The philosophy of Fouillée and his school did not satisfy Gökalp for long. One of his friends [1] states that in 1910–11 Gökalp lectured on Fouillée with great enthusiasm, but that later he adopted Durkheim's theories "which suited his natural outlook on philosophy and sociology so well that he forgot Fouillée". What was the cause of this change?

It may be rather a rash undertaking to try to explain why a thinker has accepted or rejected a particular philosophical doctrine. There is a great risk of regarding the results of a certain influence as the original cause which brought him under that influence. In this case, however, there seems to be good reason for thinking that Gökalp turned away from Fouillée's theories mainly because they stressed the importance of the individual, the free and creative personality, as the basis of society. As Gökalp always regarded society and not the individual as the factor of prime importance in history, he never fully agreed with the Western conception of independent personality as the supreme aim of human development. Even his ideal of freedom, which he proclaimed from his early years, consists in national independence and democratic rule much more than in freedom of the individual vis-à-vis society and its institutions, such as State or Church.[2]

Gökalp criticises Fouillée for not being able to explain the nature of the values accepted in any particular society nor the reason why certain ideas become *idées-forces* and others do not. In Gökalp's opinion these shortcomings of Fouillée's theory are due to the simple fact that the French philosopher did not understand the entirely social character of the *idées-forces*. In later years he attacks Fouillée for his metaphysical and monistic leanings. Fouillée sees the source of the creative forces of man in a spiritual element which, he affirms, exists in all parts of the Cosmos, both in inorganic as well as organic nature.[3] (Gökalp refers here to the

---

[1] Ali Haydar (see Şapolyo, pp. 74–5).
[2] T., p. 38. See also pp. 54–5, *post*.
[3] K.M., 8; 14; Y.M., 27, p. 3b.

"idealistic monism" of Fouillée which eliminates the fundamental distinction between matter and spirit.) Gökalp with his positivist outlook cannot accept such a theory. In his view, all scientific truth must be based on experience or experiment only, and philosophy cannot admit anything which contradicts the findings of the positive sciences.[1] This does not mean, however, that the laws of natural science dominate all spheres of existence. The monistic attempt to apply these laws to psychological and social phenomena is doomed to failure. Moreover, it has produced a serious moral crisis by creating a false idea that it is impossible to explain and establish ethical and religious values scientifically.[2] Through this impression confidence in scientific knowledge in general was shaken and the door opened to the erroneous ideas of pragmatism and agnosticism.

Following Boutroux's pluralism,[3] Gökalp claims that the problem can be solved by rejecting the monistic principle of one and the same determinism for all phenomena. Existence is found in four stages, which, although emanating one from another, are distinct and independent of each other: matter, life, soul and society. Each of these stages is more complex and therefore, according to the law of evolution, more highly developed than the preceding one. Each of them has its own laws and determinism and, consequently, its particular science. This is the origin of the four basic sciences: physics—chemistry, biology, psychology and sociology, and in addition mathematics, dealing with quantities in all the spheres. As society is the highest of the four stages, Gökalp concludes, sociology must be regarded as the supreme form of knowledge.

[1] K.M., 2.

[2] Gökalp means rationally. He often uses the word *ilim* (science) in an enlarged sense, just as he calls philosophy what is no more than concept, principle or maxim (see, for instance, Y.M., 35, pp. 162a, 164a).

[3] The fundamentals of this doctrine are already found in the writings of Renouvier and even Comte. It is difficult to ascertain whether Gökalp took this theory directly from Boutroux or through Durkheim, Boutroux's disciple at the École Normale. The same applies to the teachings of other pre-Durkheimian sociologists quoted by Gökalp.

Here Gökalp parts company with Boutroux, who had found a gradual development from determinism to freedom in the structure of the Cosmos. Gökalp uses his theory to free the values of ethics and religion from the determinism of the lower stages of existence but not from any determinism whatsoever. On the contrary, under Durkheim's influence he stresses the determinism, albeit *sui generis*, which prevails in social life. He will merely allow that this determinism is more elastic than that dominating nature and therefore permits to man, as far as he is a social being, a certain freedom of creative activity.[1]

---

[1] Y.M., 8, p. 145a–b; 42, p. 302b; 46, pp. 382b–385c. Durkheim calls this phenomenon "contingence des forces supérieures du réel" (*Sociologie*, p. 42).

## II

# SOCIOLOGICAL CONCEPTS

### IDEAL

In Durkheim's sociology Gökalp found a reply to his central question: which are the values or ideals [1] that direct social life, what is their nature and how does their influence work?

As a positivist Gökalp cannot accept either those theories which relegate the ideal to a metaphysical world or those which picture the individual as forming the ideal in his mind and imposing it on society. In his opinion the former, while recognizing the ideal as having real existence, transfer it to a sphere beyond nature. The latter, though bringing the ideal back to earth, deprive it of reality by reducing it to something subjective and artificial. The only theory which positive science can accept as offering a proof of the objective existence of ideals is that contained in Durkheim's sociology, which regards the ethical, religious and aesthetic values as social phenomena and explains them with the help of the laws obtaining in the development of society. [2]

In the development of Gökalp's theory of the ideal two main stages are discernible. At first, in his articles published in *Türk Yurdu*, [3] he identifies the ideal with the self-knowledge of society which is born when men become aware of the existence and value

[1] From the beginning of his Constantinople period Gökalp prefers the term ideal (*mefkûre*) to value (*kıymet*). In one place (K.M., 8) he states that values are the results of ideals, a remark which may be compared with Durkheim's view that judgments express the relations between a thing and an ideal (*Sociologie*, p. 139). But mostly Gökalp uses the two terms indiscriminately (see Y.M., 34, p. 143c).

[2] K.M., 8. See Durkheim, *Division*, pp. 335–6; *Sociologie*, pp. 120–32.

[3] T., pp. 38–9, 42, 54, in which he seems largely to rely on Durkheim's article "Jugements de valeur et jugements de réalité" (in *Sociologie*, pp. 117 *sq.*, 133–7).

48

of the social group to which they belong. Such an awareness, he maintains, is mostly a sudden revelation, a historic event generally taking place in a time of serious social crisis. With the birth of this common consciousness, society understands its own nature, its origin and mission. In this way the monotheistic religions came into being, Judaism in Egyptian slavery, Christianity under Rome's tyrannical rule in Palestine, and Islam during the foreign invasion of the Arabian peninsula by various political and religious forces. In such times the ideal of nationalism too is born, as happened in France in the age of Joan of Arc and in Germany during the Napoleonic wars.

The ideal in this limited sense is a kind of hidden force, moving and directing society in all its activities. It is not an unrealizable phantasy nor an aim to be realized in the future,[1] but the product of a psychological experience of a particular society in a certain period of its development. Accordingly Gökalp translates ideal by *mefkûre*. As he explains himself,[2] he created this term from the (Arabic) word *fikr* (thought), just as the European *ideal* is derived from "idea". Previously the Turkish equivalent of ideal was *hayal*, *gaye*, *emel* or *dilek* (phantom, aim, aspiration, desire), all of which have connotations different from Gökalp's conception of ideal. *Mefkûre* was quickly accepted in the Turkish vocabulary, but has recently been superseded by the old Turkish word *ülkü*.

It is inconceivable, however, that the individuals should suddenly become conscious of their society as a distinct entity if this society had not already been in existence. In Europe, for instance, a large proletariat existed before the ideal of socialism was born. But it was without class-consciousness and therefore lacked the characteristics of a real social group. The same applies to the Turkish nation, most members of which did not recognize its

---

[1] As Gökalp thought in his early period (see G.K., 8).
[2] T., p. 42. Regarding Gökalp's definition of *ideal*, cf. Durkheim, *Division*, pp. 330–36; *Sociologie*, pp. 132–8.

3

existence before the 1908–9 revolution.[1] This consideration brought Gökalp to the conclusion that he had been mistaken when in his early writings [2] he demanded the *creation* of new values or ideals. Since these values, he writes in 1918,[3] have long existed in the soul of the people in the form of hidden longings, the only thing required is to *discover* them.

Gradually Gökalp extends the meaning of ideal. This term should not be limited to the self-knowledge of society but, as he pointed out in 1923,[4] all expressions of the "soul" of society, from fairy tales and religious beliefs to moral, legal and even economic conceptions, can become ideals. The only condition is that they should be based on those objective phenomena which Durkheim regards as the most important factors in social development, the *représentations collectives (maşerî tere'iler)*. Gökalp defines these "collective ideas" as ideas common to all members of a particular society or, more precisely, as ideas which exist in its collective consciousness (*maşerî vicdan*). Such ideas are generally connected with moral or aesthetic judgments (good or bad, holy or profane, beautiful or ugly, etc.). But they become real ideals only if they are accompanied by strong emotions, such as are evoked in a time of social crisis. Ideals can therefore be defined as emotionally intensified collective ideas.[5]

This definition is not of much value as long as the origin of these ideas is not known. Gökalp accepts Durkheim's theory that the collective ideas, and with them the ideals, are born, grow, decline and perish as the result of structural changes in society affecting its size, density, homogeneity, division of labour, etc. The key to the explanation of the ideals lies in the morphology

---

[1] T., pp. 39, 42, 54–5; E., p. 63.
[2] E.g., G. K., 2, published in 1911.
[3] Y.M., 27, p. 1a.
[4] E., p. 64.
[5] E., pp. 63–6. Compare Durkheim's definition: "Ces idéaux, ce sont tout simplement les idées dans lesquelles vient se peindre et se résumer la vie sociale, telle qu'elle est aux points culminants de son développement" (*Socio, logie*, p. 136). See also Durkheim, *Division*, p. 46.

of society.[1] This, however, does not mean that the historical materialist is right in regarding ideas as a mere expression of economic development, especially of changes in the technique of production, and in denying their influence on social life. Gökalp rejects this opinion for two reasons. First, he does not regard economic conditions as the only basis of social life and all the other phenomena as their consequences or "superstructure",[2] without decisive influence on its development. Gökalp attaches great importance to economic factors, particularly in modern society, but does not assign to them priority in principle over all other social forces. Just as economic conditions influence the religious, moral, cultural and political life of society, so developments in those spheres act upon economics. Secondly, direct influence on social development is not exerted by economic factors nor even by structural changes in society, but by the collective ideas or ideals, though these, it is true, are dependent on the social morphology.[3]

Since the ideal is the product of supra-individual society, it must necessarily contain a special force which secures to it domination over the will of the individual. According to Durkheim this force manifests itself in two ways. In its direct influence the ideal evokes in the soul of the individual emotions of love, enthusiasm and worship. The individual who is not influenced by this force feels its power indirectly, i.e. through the approval or disapproval by society of his actions. When, for instance, behaving contrary to the ideal, the individual arouses a hostile reaction in society, such as blame, contempt, etc., which induces him to refrain from such actions. That is to say, the ideal has

---

[1] Cf. Durkheim, *Règles*, p. 100.

[2] In Gökalp's terminology *gölge hadise*, which is a translation of the French *épiphénomène*.

[3] E., pp. 60–66; K.M., 7. In this latter respect Gökalp's "social idealism" (*içtimaî mefkûrecilik*) is not different from Marxism. Kautsky too thinks that "der Geist bewegt die Gesellschaft, aber nicht als der Herr der ökonomischen Verhältnisse, sondern als ihr Diener" (P. Barth, *Die Philosophie der Geschichte als Soziologie*, I (Leipzig, 1922), p. 737, *n*. 2).

on the one hand a force of attraction (*prestige, icaz kuvveti*) and on the other hand a force which threatens and punishes (*sanction, teyit kuvveti*).[1]

The force which compels the individual to conform to the social ideals is called by Durkheim "opinion".[2] Gökalp explains that this term is not identical with "public opinion" (*efkâr-ı âmme*) as expressed, for instance, in the press. Public opinion may err and change, it is influenced by personal and partisan considerations and is not homogeneous in any given society. The only stable force which unites all members of society and is independent of the will of the individuals is the social consciousness as revealed in the ways of thinking, feeling and acting of society. It is not public opinion but "public feelings" (*hissiyat-ı âmme*).[3] While some sociologists call this force *esprit publique*, Gökalp prefers the term which he borrowed from Islamic law, *örf*. With evident satisfaction he points out that this term has no equivalent in French. While most of Gökalp's terms are translations from that language, he has here created an original term with which he tries, as we shall see later,[4] to solve one of his central problems, the place of Muslim canon law in modern life. His basic idea is that *örf* changes with the modifications in the structure of society. Law, which is but crystallized *örf*, has therefore to change in conformity.

*Örf* means not only social consciousness, but also those values which society has accepted. In this sense Gökalp uses *örf* in the plural, so that it becomes almost an equivalent of *mefkûre* (ideal). The principal difference between *örf* and *âdet* (custom) is that

---

[1] T., pp. 41–4; I.M., 10, p. 293. Cf. Durkheim, *Règles*, pp. 6–8; *Sociologie*, pp. 61–5; *Educ. morale*, p. 107.

[2] See Durkheim, *Sociologie*, pp. 91–4.

[3] G. Le Bon distinguishes between "opinions momentanées et changeantes" and "grandes croyances permanentes" (*Psychologie des foules*, 1895, pp. 128 *sq.*), while other sociologists draw a distinction between "public opinion" and "national spirit" (Fr. Hertz, *Nationality in History and Politics* (London, 1944), p. 49).

[4] See pp. 85–8, *post*.

only those customs are called *örf* which society approves of, while on the other hand, it comprises also the innovations (*bid'at*), which are not included in *âdet*.[1]

## INDIVIDUAL AND SOCIETY

Ideals, and especially *the* ideal, i.e. the self-knowledge of society, are born in a state of collective enthusiasm (*vecid*). Dissolving in the fire of this enthusiasm, the self of the individual is absorbed into the "social personality". The individual forgets his private interests and devotes all his efforts to the good of society. In such times man, who is self-centred by nature, is prepared to offer even his life for the community and its ideals. He becomes aware of the holiness of society and feels that its spirit gives him super-human strength. By living in a condition of such intensive social consciousness the individual rises from the level of creature (*beşer*) to that of man (*insan*).[2]

The highest moral aim of man is therefore to turn his individuality (*ferdiyet*) into personality (*şahsiyet*).[3] Individuality lies in the complex of man's physical constitution, his animal and sensual nature.[4] The individual becomes a personality by throwing off the shackles of these material factors and by learning to think and act in accordance with the ideas common to the members of his society. That part of man which is not directly subject to material forces was in the past called soul. But this was only a symbolic expression for personality, which can be defined as the totality of the thoughts and feelings existing in the consciousness of society and reflected in the consciousness of the individual—in short, the ideals.[5]

---

[1] T., p. 42; I.M., 10, pp. 290–93; Y.M., 38, pp. 222c–225b; Y.H., p. 28.

[2] T., pp. 38–40; K.M., 8; 14. Compare Durkheim, *Sociologie*, pp. 85, 133–4.

[3] Y.M., 8, pp. 143a, 146b. Regarding the origin of these terms, see Y.M., 6, p. 104a.

[4] *ihtiraslar*, opposed to *duygular* (feelings) which belong to the orbit of the soul. Gökalp appears to identify individuality with the *nafs* of Muslim scholastics.

[5] Compare Durkheim, *Sociologie*, pp. 84–5, 106; *Education*, pp. 55–7.

Just as the theologians deny all common substance to soul and body, so every attempt—such as those made by the hedonists and utilitarians—to find the origin of personality in individuality is doomed to failure. Boutroux has shown that they belong to two different worlds or stages of existence. The centre of individuality is in the consciousness of the individual (*şuur*) and his emotional experiences such as joy, sorrow, fear and anger. On the other hand personality reveals itself in the social elements of the human consciousness (*vicdan*).[1] While individual consciousness—which all living beings possess—belongs to the sphere of psychology,[2] the study of personality is the exclusive concern of sociology. Psychology is not able to deal with moral, religious or aesthetic ideas and feelings, as all these are social phenomena which can be explained only by sociological methods.[3]

Following Durkheim, Gökalp holds that in a primitive society personality is little developed. With the introduction of division of labour society becomes more differentiated and the individual belongs to various social groups (political, religious, occupational, etc.) and acquires different "consciousnesses". This is the origin of the "individual personality" (*ferdî şahsiyet*) which forms its own opinions and tastes. While this new type of man came into being in Europe with the Renaissance, it has hardly yet appeared in the Turkish and other Muslim nations which have not yet entirely emerged from their mediaeval stage. Fully developed personality in a man means not only freedom from domination by his desires, but also readiness to shake off the fetters of outworn

---

[1] Both *şuur* and *vicdan* are, according to Gökalp, translations of the French "conscience" which is used in both senses (T., p. 21). Not by accident did Gökalp choose the word *vicdan*, originally meaning conscience, for collective consciousness, since it is regarded by him as the highest moral authority. To translate *vicdan*, as R. Hartmann (p. 596) does, by *Gewissen*, however, is misleading, as the Turkish term is not limited to moral values.

[2] That is, psychology of the individual, Gökalp follows Durkheim in distinguishing between this and "collective psychology" which he identifies with sociology.

[3] Y.M., 1, pp. 2b–3a; 6, p. 104b; 42, pp. 302–4. Cf. Durkheim, *Division*, p. 318, *n.* 1; *Règles*, préface, p. xvi; *Formes*, ch. VIII.

traditions and "official" opinions. The notion of *cuius regio, eius religio* [1] is rejected by every free personality. While Gökalp, in true liberal fashion, praises this attitude, he stresses the fact that even the most developed personality is but a result of social factors reflecting collective consciousness. [2]

Gökalp seems to accept the liberal notion of free personality only as far as it suits his fight against the autocracy of the Sultanate and the dogmatic spirit of traditional Islam. By nature he was a collectivist who whole-heartedly subscribed to Durkheim's principle of the supremacy of society over the individual, provided society is understood in its true meaning of the ideas and feelings of the people and not of a reactionary ruling class. Individualism, he maintains, denotes lack of ideals and leads to scepticism, moral instability and feelings of frustration and despair. The predominance of individualism in any society is a mark of its decline. Characteristic of a community in such a stage—as exemplified by Turkish society at the beginning of this century—is the increase of mental and nervous diseases and particularly of suicide. [3]

Gökalp's faith in collectivism is rooted in the Islamic tradition of fraternity and equality among the believers. Many years before he became steeped in Durkheim's theories he wrote a poem on the occasion of a Muslim feast, in which he said :

> The people who strive each for his own end
> To-day become all brethren wholeheartedly united,
> Egoism fades away, collective feeling fills their hearts. [4]

Gökalp tries to find support for his ideas in the teachings of the *Jabarīya*, the Islamic school which denies freedom of will. In this, he thinks, it is justified, because man often entertains the illusory

---

[1] Gökalp uses the Arab saying *an-nāsu ʿalā sulūki mulūkihim* (Men follow the conduct of their kings) and the slightly different Persian proverb *har chih Khusrau bi-kunad shīrīn-ast* (Whatever the King does is pleasant).

[2] Y.M., 1, p. 2b; 6, pp. 104b–105a; 8, pp. 144a–145b; 32, p. 114a–b; E., p. 54. Cf. Durkheim, *Division*, p. 400.

[3] Cf. Durkheim's Study, *Le suicide*.

[4] Ali Nüzhet, pp. 59–60.

belief that he acts according to his own will, while in fact he unwittingly obeys the ideals obtaining in his society.[1] It is interesting to note that at the same time some Islamic reformists in Turkey, such as M. Şemsettin, tried to prove that the attitude of the *Jabarīya* contradicts the spirit of true Islam.[2]

In Gökalp's demand for the merging of the individual in society and his self-annihilation for its sake one can discern the influence of a particular Islamic trend, mysticism.[3] The Ṣūfī, the Muslim mystic, strives for deliverance from selfishness, full submission to the divine will and, in the final stage, absorption in God. It is no coincidence that Gökalp calls the ideal-producing social enthusiasm *vecid*, a term used in Islamic mysticism for ecstasy. Gökalp himself is aware that he is putting new wine into old bottles. To one of his religious poems [4] he gives the sub-title "According to Social Ṣūfīsm".[5] One of its stanzas runs:

> In the bodies there is multiplicity,
> In the hearts there is unity,
> There are no individuals, there is (only) society.
> There is no God but Allah.

But this Allah is no longer the personal God of the Qur'ān or the spiritual Being of the Ṣūfī. Gökalp's God is society. To it he attributes holiness; he calls the spirit which emanates from it to the individual *tevfik* (grâce) and compares its demands to divine commandments.[6] The sanctity of human personality is explained by its being the bearer of the "collective consciousness", the soul

---

[1] T., p. 41.

[2] Peyami Safa, p. 146.

[3] This idea has been generally accepted in Islam. See, for instance, the recent speech of an Egyptian political leader, Muṣṭafā Naḥḥās Pasha: "The religion of Muhammad . . . calls to self-sacrifice and the negation of the self and the annihilation (*fanā*) of the individual in the service of society" (*Ṣawt ul-Umma*, Cairo, 3 February 1947).

[4] *Tevhid*, in K.E., p. 79.

[5] The meaning of this expression is not, as understood by M. Hartmann (XX, p. 93, *n.* 4), "die sich der gesellschaftlichen Zusammenhänge bewusste Mystik", but a mysticism of which the deity is society.

[6] T., pp. 41, 45, and the poem *Vazife* (Y.H., p. 12).

of society taking the place of the religious conception of the divine spirit.[1]

Gökalp's conception of the divinity of society derives from Durkheim. In the opinion of the French sociologist the individual has a natural feeling of dependence or inferiority vis-à-vis society and therefore subjects himself to it. This feeling is clothed by religion in concrete and symbolic forms, while science describes it in exact and precise language. "Le croyant s'incline devant Dieu, parce que c'est de Dieu qu'il croit tenir l'être, et particulièrement son être mental, son âme. Nous avons les mêmes raisons d'éprouver ce sentiment pour la collectivité."[2] When humanity becomes more mature, positive science, and sociology in particular, takes the place of religion, explaining the relations between the individual and that Highest Power which in religion is called God and in fact is society.

### NATION

On this point Gökalp modifies Durkheim's theory in a decisive and—as has rightly been pointed out [3]—rather arbitrary way. For Durkheim's *society* he substitutes *nation*, which for the French sociologist is only one of the various social groups to which modern man belongs.[4] Consequently he transfers to the nation all the divine qualities he had found in society, replacing the belief in God by the belief in the nation: nationalism has become a religion.[5]

[1] E., p. 77. Cf. Durkheim, *Sociologie*, pp. 84, 106.

[2] Durkheim, *Sociologie*, p. 108. Cf. also *Règles*, p. 150, and *Sociologie*, p. 75: "Je ne vois dans la divinité que la société transfigurée et pensée symboliquement."

[3] See Fahri, p. 36.

[4] *Educ. morale*, pp. 83 sq. Moreover Durkheim usually prefers the terms country (*patrie*) or State (*état*) to nation.

[5] This concept, which is found in the writings of the Italian nationalist thinker G. Mazzini, has also been accepted in other Muslim countries. See, for instance, the poem *Waṭan* (Fatherland) by the contemporary Persian poet Habīb Yaghmā'ī: *Ḥubb-i waṭan dīn buwad, īmān buwad* (Patriotism is religion, is faith) (quoted in A. J. Arberry, *Modern Persian Reader* (Cambridge, 1944), p. 65).

This deification of national society has most far-reaching consequences. Gökalp does not restrict himself to declaring that whatever society wills is done, but adds that all that society desires is morally good. Society as the source of all ideals is the supreme moral authority. It is furthermore the model of the highest ethical conduct; for, contrary to the selfish individual, society is prepared to make every sacrifice for the realization of its ideals.[1] The danger involved in this conception is evident. If there are no higher values than the good of a particular society, then society is not subject to any moral obligations regarding its relations to other societies. Through identifying the ideal society with the nation, Gökalp is logically bound to approve of extreme nationalism which denies all international obligations. He himself is aware of the different moral standards he sets for the individual and the nation. In his poem *Vefa* he says:

> As individuals we are not vindictive,
> But we do not forget national revenge. . . .
> As individuals and as a nation
> We show different tendencies:
> As the latter strength and aggressiveness,
> As the former endurance and patience.[2]

The only duty Gökalp imposes on the nation as well as on the individual is faithfulness.[3]

Durkheim, from whom Gökalp takes the theory of society as the highest moral authority,[4] is not unmindful of the danger mentioned above. He points out that just as the only force which can restrain the egotism of the individual is the social group, so

---

[1] K.M., 8. Gökalp seems here to be directly influenced by Gustave Le Bon whose writings he studied. Cf. G. Le Bon, *Psychologie du socialisme* (Paris, 1912), pp. 108–9: "L'individu a presque toujours pour guide son intérêt personnel, alors que les foules obéissent le plus souvent à des intérêts collectifs et désintéressés. . . . L'altruisme profond . . . est une vertu collective."

[2] Y.H., p. 13.

[3] This duality of moral standards is common to most nationalistic ideologies. For examples cf. Fr. Hertz, op. cit., pp. 45–6.

[4] Durkheim, *Règles*, pp. 150–51; *Sociologie*, pp. 53, 74–5; *Educ. morale*, p. 102.

there is no force to control the egotism of the groups but a larger group which comprises them. He admits that there is not yet a larger organized society than the country or State and that humanity still lacks the common consciousness and common ideals necessary to constitute a real society. But he regards international society as of higher moral dignity than the nation and envisages a development towards ever larger social groups.[1] At present the only way to reconcile nationalism and cosmopolitism is the emergence of a morally restrained and "spiritualized" patriotism.[2] Durkheim's rather vague and sometimes naïvely optimistic views enabled the advocates of nationalism to find support for their theories in his writings, particularly of the time of the First World War. "The idea of 'The Nation is God' is a clear conclusion which can be drawn from Durkheim's writings, but . . . it constitutes the supreme ideal only as far as . . . the idea of humanity is realized in it."[3] This reservation was not accepted by Gökalp who, as will be shown farther on, looks with suspicion at all ideas of internationalism.

Gökalp's belief in the nation as the perfect society is found in his early writings. In his article *Yeni Hayat ve Yeni Kıymetler*, published in 1911, he makes the statement that "humanity finds its expression to-day in the notion of nationality".[4] When he became acquainted with Durkheim's theories he accepted them for two main reasons: first, in order to obtain scientific support for his belief that the nation is indeed the highest stage in human development up to the present; and second, in order to ascertain which stage of development the Turkish nation had reached,

[1] Durkheim, *Division*, pp. 265–6, 401–2; *Educ. morale*, pp. 85–9.

[2] "La patrie, telle que la réclame la conscience moderne, ce n'est pas l'État jaloux et égoïste, qui ne connaît d'autres règles que son intérêt propre, qui se considère comme affranchi de toute discipline morale" (*Educ. morale*, pp. 91–2). Compare also Durkheim's views expressed at a meeting of the Société de Philosophie in 1907 (quoted in H. Massis, *La guerre de trente ans* (Paris, 1940), pp. 41–6).

[3] M. M. Mitchell, *Emile Durkheim and the Philosophy of Nationalism* (in *Political Science Quarterly*, XLVI (1931), pp. 87–106).

[4] Y.M., 25, p. 484a.

which of its cultural values and social institutions were outworn [1]
and ought therefore to be abolished, and which of them were in
harmony with its present stage and should in consequence be
maintained and developed.[2]

From Durkheim's school [3] Gökalp borrows the theory that
society passes historically through four main stages: primitive or
tribal society (*aşiret*), society based on ethnical affinity (*kavım*),
society with a common religion (*ümmet*) and society united by
culture (*millet*).[4]

Gökalp's deep interest in the history of the ancient Turks leads
him to discourse at great length on the nature of primitive society
and its transition to the earliest form of state, based on ethnical
affinity (*kavım*). In this society racial origin is a decisive factor, as
shown by the predominance of the Arabs in the early Islamic
State. Society next passes into the theocratic state ruled by an
autocratic prince and according to divine law. Gradually the
privileges of noble birth are abolished and individuals of foreign
origin are allowed to occupy the highest positions in the Government and the Army. Gökalp illustrates this transition by the
example of the *Mawālī*, the non-Arab Muslims who obtained full
equality in the early Baghdad caliphate and rose to the highest
ranks. Similar opportunities were given to the Christians who
under the *Devşirme* system were as children forcibly converted to
Islam and pressed into the military or Court service of the Ottoman
Sultans. The foundation of this form of society is community of
religion (*ümmet*). Religion, however, is no longer the creed of a
particular people but tends to become "catholic", international.

---

[1] In Gökalp's words *peszinde*, which in his opinion is identical with *marazî*
(pathological).—Cf. Durkheim, *Règles*, III.

[2] M.T.M., 2, p. 204.

[3] As pointed out by Gökalp himself in M.T.M., 2, pp. 200, 205.

[4] Y.M., 38, p. 225b. In M.T.M. (2, p. 198) of 1915 there is no mention yet
of the stage of *kavım* which Gökalp includes in his articles published in 1918
in Y.M. In his latest writings (1923) he returns to the division into three stages
only, that is *cemia*, *camia* and *cemiyet*, which correspond to the above-mentioned
stages without the *kavım* (E., p. 70). Cf. also K.M., 33.

This society is based economically on the village, since in the meantime the tribes have become sedentary. During this process they have lost their freedom and independence and have become subject to local rulers, the owners of their land. The feudal system is typical of this social form which existed in the Orient in the time of the Abbasids, of the Seljuqs and of the Ottoman Empire.[1]

The climax of social development is the nation (*millet*), in which the "individual personality" revolts against theocratic and feudal rule as well as against obsolete religious traditions. With the strengthening of national consciousness society fights also for its external independence, thus bringing about the dissolution of multi-national empires. This national democratic and independent State is, however, not yet the ideal form of society. In the final stage of development the economic class distinctions (*sınıf*) which prevent the enjoyment of full equality by all citizens have to be abolished and society has to be organized on the basis of occupational groups or guilds (*meslek*). This is the true form of social democracy.[2]

In these views Gökalp was certainly influenced by the great social changes which took place during the 1914–18 war in most countries of Europe, and particularly in Russia. Previously he had dreamt of another form of an ideal society. In 1915 he writes [3] that the democratic State will be succeeded by a higher society in which the supreme controlling force will be not the Government, however democratic it may be, but national culture (*harsî millet*). Such a society would regard its spiritual leaders as its true representatives. Only in this form of society could moral values exercise their full influence, as the administration of justice would be entirely independent of the legislature and the executive. Although

---

[1] One of Gökalp's sweeping statements which is based on an unwarranted identification of European feudalism with the quite different structure of Muslim society in the Middle Ages.

[2] M.T.M., 2, pp. 201–2; Y.M., 33, pp. 122b–123c; 38, p. 225b; E., pp. 70–75. For particulars see chapter "Socialism and Solidarism", *post*.

[3] M.T.M., 2, pp. 202–4.

all civilized nations are advancing in this direction none of them has yet reached this ultimate stage.

Gökalp regards this form of society as the goal of social development, because it most clearly reveals the true essence of the nation, its cultural unity. He rejects all definitions of nationality based on racial or merely religious elements. Gökalp quotes many modern scientists to prove that no nation is racially homogeneous. Regarding race as a term of natural science and nation as one of social science, he denies any connection between racial origin and national character. The latter is not, as G. Le Bon holds, hereditary in a racial group, but is the result of education, i.e. the influence of social ideals. Gökalp's opposition to all racial theories is due, apart from his theoretical studies, to political considerations. In his opinion the Turks are racially more mixed than any European nation, belonging partly to the Mongolian and partly to the "white" race. But, as will be shown below, he strongly claims that all the Turks form, at least potentially, one nation. Gökalp's doubts about his own origin, which have been mentioned before, may have further strengthened his conviction that nationality has nothing to do with race.

Political unity too cannot serve as a basis of nationality. Gökalp regards the population of Switzerland as being composed of three different nations and rejects, except in his early writings, the idea of all Ottoman citizens constituting one nation. "The clearly expressed will to continue a life in common", which is for E. Renan [1] one of the main marks of nationality, is not mentioned in Gökalp's definition of a nation. For him the ideals which unite a nation imply common cultural heritage rather than political will to build a common future. Finally, Gökalp is opposed to the traditional conception of Islam that all Muslims form one *millet*. He uses this term, which originally means religious community, in the modern sense of nation, while calling the international Islamic community *ümmet*.

[1] *Qu'est-ce qu'une nation?* (Paris, 1882).

Gökalp's own definition of a nation is: a society consisting of people who speak the same language, have had the same education and are united in their religious, moral and aesthetic ideals—in short, those who have a common culture and religion.[1] A similar definition is given in the 1931 programme of the Republican People's Party, the party in power in modern Turkey: "The nation is a political and social body composed of citizens who are bound together by unity of language, culture and ideal." The element of religion has significantly been dropped.[2]

### CULTURE AND CIVILIZATION

Having found the basis of nationality to be in culture, Gökalp is at pains to define this term. He is aware that every nation possesses spiritual and material values which are not peculiar to it but are common to different nations. Such values are excluded from culture (*hars*),[3] which in Gökalp's definition is entirely national, and are called civilization (*medeniyet*), to which an international character is attributed. The distinction between these two terms, which play a major rôle in Gökalp's theories, is mainly formal. Gökalp regards as part of culture all feelings, judgments and ideals, while rational and scientific knowledge, methods and technology are considered as belonging to civilization. This definition leads him to give culture an emotional and subjective character. On the other hand, values of civilization have mainly an intellectual, objective, practical and often material character. Cultural values grow in the subconscious of society,

---

[1] T., pp. 50–51; Y.M., 51, p. 482b; 62, pp. 182–5; 70, p. 53a–c; E., pp. 15–20.

[2] *Tarih*, the semi-official textbook of History for Turkish schools, IV (Istanbul, 1934), p. 180.

[3] This term was formed by Gökalp from an Arabic root as an exact equivalent of the French *culture*. The word *hars* was soon accepted into the Turkish vocabulary but has recently been largely replaced by *kültür*. Before Gökalp defined culture as the totality of national values, he used the word *irfan* (K.E., pp. 24, 125) or *medeniyet* (K.E., p. 22) in the same sense without distinguishing between culture and civilization (see G.K., 8). However, from 1918 onwards he makes a clear distinction between *hars* (culture), *irfan* (knowledge or education in a general sense) and *medeniyet* (civilization) (Y.M. 27, p. 1a; Y.M., 33, p. 123a).

while their counterparts in civilization are formed and developed consciously.

Here, as in so many of Gökalp's definitions, his emotional and biased approach is fully revealed. He usually attributes to culture praiseworthy and attractive qualities such as originality, simplicity, spontaneity, beauty, etc. To civilization are assigned the opposite attributes. This unscientific treatment reflects Gökalp's inner struggle between heart and reason, between what he likes or loves, and what he accepts or is compelled to accept by his intellect. Another reason for his attitude can be found in the historical circumstances which this theory is designed to explain. As will be seen later, Gökalp regards the Turks as rich in culture but poor in civilization. He therefore tries to emphasize the importance of culture and to warn his countrymen of the pitfalls of civilization. Culture, he claims, when finding its expression in strong national ideals, is more powerful than civilization. He quotes history to prove that nations with a mature culture defeated their enemies even if those had reached a higher stage of civilization.

When discussing the respective contents of culture and civilization Gökalp points out that the language, art, law, ethics and even religion of a particular nation belong partly to its cultural heritage and partly to international civilization. The popular literature written in the language of the masses, for instance, forms part of the culture of a given society, while "highbrow" literature, reflecting a certain civilization, is common to the upper classes of different nations. As an example, Gökalp contrasts the simple Turkish poems of Yunus Emre, the popular mystic, with the refined Persian poems of Jalāl ud-DīnRūmī, also a mystic of alleged Turkish origin who lived for one part of his life in Anatolia.[1]

Gökalp's parallel antitheses between culture and civilization—national and international, and emotional and intellectual—are not always compatible with each other and lead him to doubtful and

[1] T., pp. 19–23; Y.M., 27, p. 3a; 60, pp. 142a–143b; 61, pp. 162c–163a; 62, p. 184c; E., pp. 27–37; Y.H., p. 45; T.M.T., p. 7.

sometimes clearly mistaken interpretations of historical phenomena. There can be little doubt that civilization has values based
on emotions, as proved by no one better than by Rūmī to whom
Gökalp himself refers. Only a writer who, like Gökalp, had an
insufficient understanding of Western civilization could say that
all that the artists of the Renaissance inherited from classical
Greece and Rome was form and technique, while the spirit of
their creations was that of their national traditions.[1]

Different national cultures, Gökalp writes, can form part of one
civilization, as is shown by the fact that Western civilization is
common to the English, French and Germans and has even been
adopted by the Jews and Japanese. While civilization is an assimilating factor between nations, culture makes for greater differen-
tiation and variation. However, civilization cannot be regarded as
having been acquired by any nation as long as it has not been
assimilated by the popular national culture. When accepted by
the educated class alone it remains a foreign and harmful element
in the cultural life of the nation. The individual belongs to a
certain civilization only through the medium of his nation; real
civilization can only be created on the basis of developed national
cultures. This is one of Gökalp's claims which are not based on
historical or sociological grounds but which are made for a practical
political reason : he wants his countrymen to be rooted first of all in
Turkish culture and only afterwards to adopt Western civilization.
It is noteworthy that sometimes Gökalp himself admits that
international civilization precedes national cultures which are born
from it.[2]

Values of civilization are nothing but the elements common to
different cultures. This definition leads Gökalp to one of his
fundamental theories, namely, that every nation fully maintains
its original and independent culture in the framework of the
civilization to which it belongs.[3]

[1] E., pp. 134–6.      [2] M.T.M., 2, p. 202; E., p. 90.
[3] Y.M., 27, pp. 2a–3b; 60, p. 143a; E., pp. 27, 47, 89–90. Cf. Durkheim,
*Division*, p. 265.

4

His belief in nationalism makes Gökalp overlook the decisive and
destructive influence of civilization on national culture. He admits [1]
that a nation adopting a new civilization undergoes certain
modifications of its native culture. But he ignores the fact that
civilization, and particularly modern civilization, undermines the
bases of national culture and destroys its peculiar character. It
would sometimes appear that Gökalp is not entirely unaware of
this process and is anxious that it should be combated and
arrested. Such an attitude can be explained by political motives,
although it is hardly compatible with Gökalp's own insistence on
scientific objectivity.

Durkheim takes quite a different view on this matter. He often
stresses the levelling tendency of modern civilization which is apt
to eliminate the differences between cultures.[2] This is one of the
few instances where Gökalp differs on a fundamental point from
his teacher. Gökalp's whole distinction between culture and
civilization does not exist in Durkheim's theory. The French
sociologist, and for that matter also G. Le Bon, calls both these
concepts *civilisation*, which in his words is "l'ensemble des plus
hautes valeurs humaines" or "l'ensemble d'idées, de sentiments,
de croyances et de préceptes de conduite",[3] a definition which
covers Gökalp's notion of culture. Society, which according to
Gökalp creates culture, is in Durkheim's writings [4] defined as the
"source and protector of civilization". One of its aspects in Durkheim's view is language, which to Gökalp is the most outstanding
expression of culture.

Gökalp seems to have borrowed his theory of culture and civilization, indirectly, from German sociology, perhaps from Fer-
dinand Tönnies who first published his famous *Gemeinschaft und
Gesellschaft* in 1887. Among the many sociologists quoted in
Gökalp's writings the name of Tönnies does not seem to occur.

[1] T.M.T., p. 7; Y.M., 20, p. 382a–b.
[2] See Durkheim, *Division*, pp. 106–7, 144–7.
[3] *Sociologie*, pp. 78–9.
[4] Ibid., p. 78.

Tönnies' ideas are, however, known to have influenced French sociologists whose works Gökalp studied, such as Gaston Richard who at one period belonged to Durkheim's circle. In a critical review of Tönnies' book Durkheim himself accepts the essential distinction between these two social forms with certain reservations.[1]

Tönnies regards culture as the expression of the organic society or community (*Gemeinschaft*) which is based on the "natural will" (*Wesenswille*) of its members and reflects their emotional characteristics, while the "free or arbitrary will" (*Kürwille*, originally *Willkür*), the product of the intellect to which it remains subject, creates the "artificial" society (*Gesellschaft*) and its expression, civilization. In defining these two sociological forms Tönnies might well have inspired Gökalp's whole formal distinction between culture and civilization. In the same loving terms which Gökalp applies to the society based on a common culture, Tönnies describes *Gemeinschaft* as growing organically from the people and as being based on common emotions, beliefs and traditions and on a feeling of fraternity and concord among its members.[2] This form of society existed inter alia in the guilds to which Gökalp also attaches such high importance.[3] As a result of the economic progression from agriculture and handicraft to commerce and industry a "city society" based solely on common interests comes into existence, the *Gesellschaft*.[4] Tönnies' negative attitude towards modern city life may be compared to Gökalp's criticism, explained later on,[5] of the *sehriler*, the "townsfolk", though Gökalp refers only to the upper classes, which have become estranged from the people and its culture.

Tönnies, too, regards the common people, in whom reside the forces of imagination, conscience and religious beliefs, as the bearers

---

[1] See *Revue philosophique de la France et de l'Étranger*, XXVII (1889), pp. 416–22. Cf. also P. A. Sorokin, *Contemporary Sociological Theories* (1928), p. 491, who claims that Durkheim was influenced by Tönnies.

[2] F. Tönnies, *Gemeinschaft und Gesellschaft* (6. u. 7. Aufl., Berlin, 1926), pp. 108–15, 118, 132–3, 139–40, 214–17.

[3] Ibid., p. 195.      [4] Ibid., pp. 51–3.      [5] Ibid., p. 76, *post*.

of culture, while the educated and rich [1] create civilization, the main elements of which are consciousness and intellectualism.[2] Like Gökalp, Tönnies castigates the reprehensible aspects of civilization such as selfishness, individualism, greed, etc., and deplores that in the *Gesellschaft* the peculiarities of the "natural societies" are so completely eliminated that nothing is left but the individual and the State. Tönnies regards the State as the political organ of the *Gesellschaft*. He stresses its artificial and oppressive character and even claims that "there is hardly any direct connection between State and morality."[3] This attitude appears to have influenced Gökalp who also is somewhat critical of the State.

On the other hand, the two sociologists differ fundamentally in their attitude toward " nation ". Gökalp regards it as the natural society, the bearer of culture and the source of moral values. Tönnies holds that nation (*Nation*), unlike people (*Volk*), is one of the forms of the *Gesellschaft*, which creates the State and civilization. From his experience of social conditions in Europe, which were different from those in Turkey, Tönnies deduces that modern nationalism developed hand in hand with capitalism and the industrial revolution which undermined the national cultures and created Western civilization.[4] From this he reaches the conclusion that the transition from popular culture to State civilization is an inevitable decline in the life of every nation,[5] an idea which Spengler later elaborated in his *Untergang des Abendlandes*. Gökalp, on the other hand, who, with all his romanticism, is far from taking such a pessimistic view, believes that culture and civilization are compatible and jointly determine the life of modern nations.[6]

---

[1] F. Tönnies, *Gemeinschaft und Gesellschaft* (6. u. 7. Aufl., Berlin, 1926), p. 242.

[2] Ibid., pp. 140, 152–3, 241.      [3] Ibid., pp. 227–9, 245.
[4] Ibid., pp. 164, 239–40, 247.      [5] Ibid., p. 239.

[6] In addition, Tönnies differs from Gökalp in his metaphysical approach and his starting-point, which is the psychology of the individual.

## COMMON PEOPLE AND ÉLITE

Like Tönnies and the adherents of romanticism from Rousseau and Herder to Gustave Le Bon, Gökalp finds the source of culture and ideals in the "common people" (*halk*).[1] In his opinion, however, the people is only the raw material from which the "nation" (*millet*) is formed.[2] In the old Ottoman Empire the people consisted of the subjects of an autocratic ruler (*raiye*), the ignorant masses (*avam*). Gökalp does not share the attitude of contempt for the masses implied in these terms, but on the other hand he also rejects the Marxist view which identifies the people with the proletariat only. In his opinion everybody, without distinction of class and education, is one of the people, on condition that he recognizes the equality of everyone before the law. On the basis of this definition Gökalp excludes from the people the aristocracy and feudal lords, but includes the middle class and intelligentsia as long as they do not claim any special privileges.

Regarding the aloofness of the educated as one of the factors most detrimental to national well-being, he points out that any intelligentsia which isolates itself from the people undermines national culture and substitutes for it a foreign civilization. Thus a gulf of mutual misunderstanding and hostility is opened between the educated and the people. To prevent this danger to national unity, it is incumbent on the educated "to go to the people"[3] and to learn from it the foundations of national culture. In this way they can perform their duty of bringing the subconscious emotions and ideas of the people to light. In a backward country like Turkey the educated have also to bring modern civilization

---

[1] See his poem in K.E., p. 80: "Hakkın muradı halktan fırladı", a kind of equivalent to *vox populi, vox dei*.

[2] Cf. the similar distinction in French between *peuple* which means either "the masses of the population . . . or else a community united by a common origin" and *nation* which "tends to be used . . . in the purely political sense" (Royal Inst. of Internat. Affairs, *Nationalism* (1939), p. xviii).

[3] The slogan *Halka doğru* (Towards the People), which is frequently found in Gökalp's articles, is certainly an echo of the famous Russian movement of "Going to the People" in the second half of the nineteenth century.

to the masses. Only by fulfilling both these tasks do the educated
in fact become the élite (*güzideler*) of the nation, forming a spiritual
Government in relation to which the political leaders appear only
as executive organs.[1] From this conception of élite is derived
Gökalp's idea of the Leader as the figure in which the consciousness of society crystallizes. Although Gökalp in a later period
admitted the need of a leader in certain circumstances, he did
not follow the example of Le Bon [2] in working out this idea
theoretically.

The great artists (geniuses, *dahiler*, in Gökalp's terminology)
also are only the representatives of the people, whose feelings and
character they express. Although all popular creations are in
Gökalp's opinion original (and therefore natural, beautiful, etc.),
they are mostly primitive and imperfect technically. Therefore,
the great artist has to effect a synthesis of the popular culture of
his nation with the artistic traditions of other nations which have
reached a higher stage of aesthetic development.[3]

The examples Gökalp quotes to prove this theory show how
dangerous generalizations of this kind are. The anecdotes of
*Nasrettin Hoca*, the mystical hymns by Yunus Emre, the Turkish
architecture, calligraphy, pottery, etc., have all been influenced by
the art of other nations to an extent that they can hardly be called
original. The belief that the artistic expressions of the common
people are primitive only in form and the importance attached to
national traditions in the formation of the genius are typical of the
romantic school of nationalism.

---

[1] See Gökalp's lecture, *Halk ve Güzideler*, quoted in Şapolyo, pp. 119–23;
see also Y.H., p. 21; E., pp. 41–2. Cf. Georges Sorel's philosophy of history
"which sharply emphasizes the significance of the élite as the embodiment of
the genius of a people." (*Enc. of Social Sciences*, VI, p. 134).

[2] *Psychologie des foules*, pp. 103 *sq.*

[3] Şapolyo, p. 200; Y.M., 34, p. 144a; E., pp. 42–3; K.M., 3.

# III

# WESTERNIZATION

## OTTOMANISM

The beginning of Gökalp's literary activities coincided with a period of major political and intellectual crises in Turkish history. Those were the days of the *Meşrutiyet*, the constitutional régime founded by the Young Turks after the 1908–9 revolution. The Turkish intelligentsia was torn between three conflicting ideologies: the liberalism of the *Tanzimat* period, which demanded assimilation to the West and hoped to save the multi-national Ottoman Empire by granting equal rights to all its citizens without distinction of religion and race (*Ottomanism*); the clericalism of the orthodox Muslims who insisted that Islam must retain its dominating influence on politics, culture and social life and serve as an indissoluble link between the Muslim nations inside the Empire, particularly Turks and Arabs, and those beyond its borders (*Islamism* or *Pan-Islamism*); and Turkish nationalism which in its first, romantic period fought for closer relations between all peoples of Turkish race in the hope of eventually uniting them in one Empire (*Pan-Turkism* or *Turanism*).

After some hesitation Gökalp rejected the first two ideals and supported the Turanian movement. With the change of political circumstances, however, he took exception to its extreme aims and developed his own ideology which he called Turkism (*Türkçülük*) and which is in fact a kind of synthesis of the trends mentioned above with the emphasis on the element of nationalism.

Like most members of his party, Union and Progress,[1] Gökalp in the beginning favoured Ottomanism (*Osmanlıcılık*). In an article

[1] See the Statutes (*nizamname*) of the Committee of Union and Progress of 25 November (8 December) 1908 (*Oriente Mod.*, XXIII (1943), p. 371).

published in 1911 [1] he points out that the social revolution which was so urgently needed and its concomitant transformation of values could only be born out of the Ottoman spirit. Already in these days, however, he calls the future national culture [2] sometimes Ottoman and sometimes Turkish. During the last years before the outbreak of the First World War he further clarified his attitude. In his writings of 1913 he still favours the existence of a multi-national Ottoman State. But he rejects the attempts of the *Tanzimat* period to maintain the unity of the Empire and to gain the sympathy of the Western Powers by creating an Ottoman nation composed of the different national and religious communities. He strongly disagrees with the view of the advocates of Ottomanism that all the subjects of one State are members of the same nation. This, in Gökalp's opinion, is the ideal, but unfortunately it does not exist in the Ottoman Empire with its mixed population. Finally, since culture, as defined by Gökalp, postulates a homogeneous national society, every attempt to develop an Ottoman culture is self-contradictory. [3]

After a short time Gökalp began to doubt the value of Ottomanism even as a political ideal. The enthusiastic spirit of fraternity among all the communities, which prevailed in the first months after the revolution of the Young Turks, [4] quickly cooled down. The desire for national independence had become so strong that mere promises of equal treatment by the new rulers could no longer imbue the Christian and even the non-Turkish Muslim subjects of the Sultan with loyalty to the Ottoman State. This was strikingly proved by the Albanian revolt and the Balkan wars

---

[1] *Yeni Hayat ve Yeni Kıymetler* (G.K., 8).

[2] Here Gökalp uses still the term *medeniyet*, the meaning of which in later days he limits to civilization (see his later critical remarks on this article in Y.M., 27, p. 1a).

[3] T., pp. 7, 29–31, 50–51; see also E., p. 18.

[4] Gökalp rightly remarks that this French term (*Jeunes Turcs*) is misleading and that it would be preferable to call them, as was the habit in Namık Kemal's days, " New Ottomans " (*Yeni Osmanlılar*), since they—contrary to the Turkists—wanted to form one nation of the citizens of the Ottoman Empire only, but of *all* its citizens (Y.M., 51, p. 482b).

(1912–13), as a result of which the Turks lost almost all their European provinces. The lesson was not lost on Gökalp. In 1914 he writes that a State can exist only if based on one nation, since men belonging to different nations cannot love the same fatherland.[1] In the present wave of nationalism multi-national empires are doomed and there is no way of preventing the dissolution of the Ottoman State.[2]

Gökalp does not base these views only on the lessons of history. With astonishing frankness he admits as early as 1913 that the *Tanzimat* leaders and Young Turks were not sincere in their recognition of the national rights of the various communities, but used the ideal of Ottomanism as a cloak for the Turkification of the State. Just as they called the official and literary language Ottoman although it was fundamentally nothing but Turkish, they tried—without admitting it—to give the Turks a dominating position in all spheres of life. No wonder that the reaction of the non-Turks was to strengthen their national movements. Thus Ottomanism not only did not unite the different communities, but even increased their hostility to the Young Turk Government.[3]

The greatest sufferers from Ottomanism were, however, the Turks themselves, who were led by it to discard the only ideal which could save them from complete ruin—nationalism. As the Turks lacked national consciousness in the modern sense, they were not aware of the decline in their power which had resulted from the social and economic developments of the last few generations. In particular they did not sufficiently appreciate the detrimental effect of the gradual occupation by the Christians and Jews of economic key positions in commerce, industry and the professions. The Muslims who formed the ruling element of the population remained only peasants, Government officials and

[1] T., p. 58. It is interesting to note that Durkheim too, during the 1914–18 war, reached the conclusion that "cette volonté commune (des membres d'une nationalité) . . . est même le seul fondement solide des États" (*L'Allemagne*, p. 40).

[2] E., p. 38.          [3] T., pp. 29–30.

soldiers. While "the poor Turks inherited from the Ottoman Empire nothing but a broken sword and an old-fashioned plough,"[1] there arose among the non-Muslim communities, which had no part in the Government, a wealthy bourgeoisie with European education. The Muslims produced no such class possessing the qualifications required of rulers, notably education, initiative and organizing abilities. Gökalp considers this abnormal situation one of the main causes of the downfall of the Ottoman Empire.[2]

There is certainly much truth in Gökalp's analysis. But he disregards two of the main reasons for the economic backwardness of the Turks as compared with their non-Muslim compatriots: the Ottoman tradition stigmatizing commerce and industry as undignified occupations, unworthy of the ruling class; and the closer contacts of the Christian and Jewish communities with Western Europe.

### FAILURE OF THE "TANZIMAT"

Gökalp does not confine his criticism of the *Tanzimat* period to its political and economic mistakes. In his opinion the leaders of this movement and their Young Turk followers also failed to solve the cultural problems of the country. The *Tanzimat* intelligentsia was mainly of the *hezarfen* type, dilettants who lacked expert knowledge on any of the multifarious subjects dealt with in their writings.[3] However, Gökalp's explanation that this phenomenon was merely the result of the economic and social backwardness of Turkey is not convincing. Such dilletantism existed in the period of Enlightenment of many nations. Like the writers of similar periods in Europe, the Turkish educated class made use of the newly acquired freedom of thought and expression to try out the rational approach to every subject. Furthermore, as teachers of the masses the modern intelligentsia had to deal with a great number of different subjects, translating and popularizing the ideas of the West.

---

[1] E., p. 71.          [2] T., pp. 4–6; E., pp. 71, 80.          [3] K.M., 7.

The *Tanzimat* leaders, Gökalp says, recognized that to save the Empire from its external foes reforms had to be introduced in the military organization, judicial system, economic structure and methods of education. But they never tried to make clear to themselves what should be accepted from Europe and what should be taken from the national tradition. One of their most serious deficiencies was that they did not fully understand Western civilization. Most of them derived their knowledge of it from their intercourse with the Levantine population of the Beyoğlu (Pera) quarter of Constantinople.[1] They therefore imitated mainly the external, and often inferior, aspects of European civilization, without penetrating to its philosophical and scientific foundations. In the economic field they introduced a number of new fashions in dress, food, building, furnishings and other articles of consumption, but did not adopt Western methods of production. The result was that the traditional crafts decayed without even the nucleus of a modern industry being formed.[2]

The *Tanzimat* leaders did not take proper account of the differences in the elements which they tried to combine. This lack of system, Gökalp writes, led them into a double error. Where they did reform, they were not radical enough and stopped half-way. On the other hand, where they assimilated to the West, they went too far and tried to introduce innovations which the Turkish people would not accept, as they were entirely foreign to them. During the *Tanzimat* period Western subjects were introduced in several schools, but the *medrese* (religious college) and other traditional institutions were not touched. The judicial machinery was tinkered with but not altered fundamentally. As a result, a dangerous dualism in all public and cultural life was created.

---

[1] Cf. the excellent description of the *züppe*, the superficially Europeanized Turkish snob of those days, in the writings of Hüseyin Rahmi (*Mürebbiye, Şık,* etc.) and in Halide Edib's novel *Sinekli Bakkal* (first published in English under the title of *The Clown and His Daughter*, London, 1935).

[2] This process had already commenced in the eighteenth century (cf. de Volney, *Voyage en Egypte et en Syrie pendant les années* 1783, 1784 *et* 1785).

Institutions belonging to two different civilizations, the mediaeval
Oriental and the modern European, existed side by side. The only
exceptions were two institutions in which the European system
was adopted thoroughly and which therefore were highly successful, the Military Academy (*Harbiye*) and the Faculty of Medicine
(*Tıbbiye*) in Constantinople. All the other schools suffered from
the clash between the traditional and the modern outlook, and the
students acquired neither a good Oriental nor an all-round
Western education.[1]

By accepting European ideas and values indiscriminately and
without regard to the condition of the Turkish people, the
*Tanzimat* failed to solve the central problem of Turkish culture,
the contrast between the masses and the intelligentsia or "élite".[2]
A deep gulf, which had existed for hundreds of years,[3] divided
the common people from the Court, the *ulema* (clergy) and the
officials. The last-mentioned, called *şehriler* (townsfolk) since they
were concentrated in the capital, were largely of foreign origin
and looked with undisguised contempt on the masses of the people,
particularly the provincials (*taşralılar*). In more recent time they
became the deadly foes of the national movement. They regarded
the name "Turk" as a derogatory word meaning rude, uneducated
villager. In proof of this statement Gökalp quotes a number of
proverbs which in his opinion originated from these circles: "When
a Turk gets on a horse, he regards himself as a *Bey* (nobleman)."—
"Give a Turk the title *Bey*, his first act will be to kill his father."
—"The Turk gets wise after the event."[4]

The élite, he adds, created civilization out of Byzantine and a
Arab-Persian elements, and the common people had no part in
it. The Court poets, who are regarded as the Ottoman classics,

---

[1] T., p. 36; Y.M., 27, pp. 1b–2b; 60, p. 143a–b; E., pp. 48, 56–7.

[2] See the chapter "Common People and Elite", *ante*.

[3] Gökalp finds it already in the time of Seljuq rule in Anatolia, where
popular Turkish poetry was sharply contrasted with that of refined writers in
Persian, the cultural representatives of "society" (Y.M., 60, p. 142a).

[4] T., pp. 26–8.

wrote in a language incomprehensible to the masses, as they used a large number of Arabic and Persian words and expressions. In all spheres of culture (literature, music, moral values and even religious beliefs) the two classes, the rulers and the people, diverged completely.[1]

The period of *Tanzimat* and Ottomanism did not bring any change in this situation. The gulf between the élite and the people, between the "civilization" of the rulers and the "culture" of the masses, was not bridged. With the penetration of European ideas into Turkey a new intelligentsia was formed which gradually undermined the influence of the Court and the clergy. Even the leaders of the Enlightenment, however, did not favour the ideal of political and cultural nationalism. They did not understand that it was impossible to introduce a new civilization, the European, before national culture had been so fully developed that it could assimilate the new values without losing its own peculiar character. No wonder, therefore, that they failed to make their ideas acceptable to the common people. The masses did not adopt European civilization any more than they had in the past adopted the Oriental civilization of the ruling classes. The poetry of *Servet-i Fünun*, the leading literary school at the end of the Hamidian period, clearly shows the estrangement of the educated class from the people, its interests and taste. The general public did not take to the creations of this school because they were no less artificial and remote from everyday life than the classical *Divan* literature. This was not only because of their language and form. It was the cosmopolitan attitude and exaggerated individualism of the Turkish intelligentsia of those days which were entirely strange to the masses of the people.[2]

Gökalp's judgment of the *Tanzimat* period and its influence is one-sided. Like every initiator of a new movement, he exaggerates the deficiencies of the preceding period. He does not seem to be

[1] E., pp. 29–35.
[2] Y.M., 1, pp. 3a–b; 27, pp. 1b–3b; 42, p. 303c; 60, p. 143a–b; E., pp. 89–90.

aware of the fact that in many respects he himself only elaborated
ideas which had first been conceived by the Turkish modernists
of the *Tanzimat* and early Hamidian period. Political freedom and
patriotism had been proclaimed by Namık Kemal and the principles of evolution and progress by Tevfik Fikret. Abdulhak Hamit
had advocated the transformation of Islam into a purely ethical
religion, and both he and Fikret had demanded the emancipation
of women. Gökalp sometimes [1] admits that the *Tanzimat* introduced valuable innovations which brought the Turks nearer to
democracy and modern civilization. But in general he does not
sufficiently appreciate the importance of this period which, in spite
of all its imperfections, was a necessary stage in the modern
development of his nation.

### PROPER WESTERNIZATION

Gökalp concurs in the fundamental idea of the *Tanzimat* that
Turkey should learn from the West. In his early writings there
are still signs of a Muslim feeling of superiority which for so long
prevented his co-religionists from admitting the high material
development of the West and the necessity of learning from it.
In an article which he published in 1911 in the periodical *Genç
Kalemler* [2] he sneers at the non-Muslim minorities in Turkey who
accepted European civilization unquestioningly, "just like a man
who buys ready-made suits." But "we Muslims", he adds, "cannot, owing to the particular style of our life, imitate fixed models
of civilization. We need clothes made to measure, principles of
life which fit our figure. We have to create a new civilization from
our own spirit. . . . This national Ottoman civilization will arouse
the envy of European civilization." In his national enthusiasm
Gökalp finds support in Nietzsche's tirades against Western
civilization. He declares that this civilization "is based on rotten
and decaying foundations and is doomed to ruin. The new civilization will be created by the Turkish race which has not, like other

---

[1] Y.M., 32, p. 104a–b; 36, p. 181a.          [2] G.K., 8.

races, been demoralized by alcohol and licentious living, but has
been strengthened and rejuvenated in glorious wars ". In his poem
*The New Attila*, which he wrote during the Balkan wars, Gökalp
warns Europe of the military power of the Turks who will defeat
them as the Huns, their ancestors, did before.[1]

Gökalp did not hold these views for long. The defeat of the
Ottoman Empire in the Tripoli and Balkan wars made him pain-
fully aware that European civilization must not be underrated.
He began to understand that the *Tanzimat* leaders were right in
saying that the Turks could not hold back their enemies if they
did not learn from them. In his poem *Esnaf Destanı* he says:

> We were defeated because we were so backward,
> To take revenge, we shall adopt the enemy's science.
> We shall learn his skill, steal his methods.
>
> On progress we will set our heart.
> We shall skip five hundred years
> And not stand still. Little time is left.[2]

Gökalp finally came to the conclusion that the spread of
Western civilization to Turkey was a historical necessity. After this
civilization had pervaded Russia since Peter the Great and later
the Balkan countries, the time had now come for the Ottoman
Turks to accept it and thus bid farewell to Oriental civilization.[3]

Gökalp does not regret this development. He regards Oriental
civilization as foreign to the Turkish spirit and therefore does not
consider the adoption of another civilization as detrimental.
Oriental civilization had never been absorbed by more than a thin
layer of the ruling classes. Furthermore, it was in his opinion not
really connected with Islam, the religion of the Turks. To call it
Islamic civilization is a mistake which arose from the fact that the
Ottoman Turks received it from Muslim nations, the Persians and
the Arabs. In fact it was nothing but the continuation of Byzantine
civilization, exactly as Western civilization is fundamentally not
Christian but the offspring of Roman civilization. The foundations

---

[1] K.E., pp. 90–92.    [2] K.E., pp. 123–4.    [3] E., pp. 38–40, 55.

of Oriental civilization in the spheres of philosophy, medicine, science and art are mostly derived from the Graeco-Roman-Byzantine heritage. Oriental music which is cultivated by Muslims, Greek-Orthodox, Armenians and Jews alike well illustrates this common pre-Islamic origin. In the Middle Ages, Western and Eastern civilization developed on parallel lines. But with the Renaissance and Reformation Europe embarked on a new course which gave it a marked superiority over the stagnant East. The introduction of the division of labour, which is, according to Durkheim, the decisive factor in the growth of modern civilization, created in Europe a new mentality, breaking the shackles of tradition and opening a period of progress and creative activity. The peoples of the East, however, remained fast bound to mediaeval traditions, until they too began to accept the ideas of Western civilization.[1]

Contrary to the *Tanzimat* leaders, Gökalp demands the acceptance of Western *civilization* in full. On the other hand, he disagrees with the advocates of an exaggerated Westernization and warns the Turks not to borrow from Europe what is not civilization but belongs to the sphere of *culture*. His distinction between culture and civilization serves Gökalp as a touchstone to determine what is and what is not to be accepted from the West. As mentioned above, civilization, which is by nature international, covers only scientific methods, the natural sciences and technical processes. All these should be adopted from Europe. All spiritual values, however, are part of culture which should not be borrowed from other nations but should be taken from the religious and national heritage.[2] In his last years Gökalp defined his views on this matter in a conversation with his disciple Enver Behnan Şapolyo. He strongly objected to Şapolyo's plan of going to Europe to study history there. In his opinion it would be a mistake to study the humanities (including his own subject, sociology, which he took entirely from Western sources) in Europe, since most

---

[1] E., pp. 38–9, 51–5.
[2] T., pp. 9, 18–19, 35, 37.

Western university teachers are "missionaries" who seduce the young Turkish student and turn him into a kind of interpreter of views foreign to his national culture. The young Turk should study only natural sciences and technical subjects with Western teachers and learn the modern scientific methods, as Gökalp did himself, from European literature.[1]

Only a man like Gökalp who had never visited Europe and whose understanding of its culture was limited could ignore the strong ties linking the humanities with natural sciences generally and the spiritual culture of the West with its material achievements, which he calls civilization, in particular. He occasionally admits [2] that the philosophical, aesthetic and moral teachings of Western civilization will have a beneficial influence on the Turks. But the only rôle he allots to this influence is to destroy the foreign traditions which the Turks accepted in the past, mainly from Persia. With an astounding naïveté he thinks that it would be possible to limit the influence of Western civilization and to prevent it from penetrating into those spheres which he regards as the exclusive field of national culture. The cultural development in Turkey after Gökalp's death proves that the process of Westernization is not limited to the sphere of "civilization" in his own sense of the word but covers the whole life of the nation.

[1] Şapolyo, p. 159.
[2] Y.M., 60, p. 143a–c.

# IV

# ISLAM

## GÖKALP'S ATTITUDE TOWARD RELIGION

Gökalp regards Islam, as well as any other religion, as a historical phenomenon subject to change and dependent on the social circumstances in which it developed. This approach was revolutionary in his days. To explain Islam by comparison with similar phenomena in other religions [1] was a daring thing to do at a time when Muslim fanaticism was still strong in Turkey. But for the anti-Islamic attitude of Atatürk, Gökalp might have become the initiator of a fruitful scientific investigation of Islam in Turkey and perhaps even the father of an interesting religious reform movement.

Like most of his Muslim contemporaries Gökalp was educated in a traditional spirit. His early emotional and intellectual outlook was formed by religion.[2] However, under the influence of mysticism (Ṣūfism) on the one hand and of rationalism on the other he turned away from orthodox Islam, its beliefs and obligations. He was able to rationalize to his satisfaction some religious observances, and to others he tried to give a new meaning while keeping their external forms.

Among the first writings of Gökalp there are three poems, published in the Diyarbekir paper *Dicle* [3] on the occasion of Şeker *Bairamı* (the feast of the end of Ramadān, the month of fast), in

---

[1] See, for instance, Y.M., 6, pp. 102b–104a.

[2] It may be no mere coincidence that Gökalp's teacher Durkheim also "was fully conscious of his own predominantly ethical and religious preoccupations and frequently had occasion to recall to his colleagues . . . that he was, after all, the son of a Rabbi" (H. Alpert, *Emile Durkheim and His Sociology*, New York, 1939, p. 15).

[3] Quoted in Ali Nüzhet, pp. 58–60.

which he praises the daily prayers, the religious alms (*zekât*) and the feast. In these poems Gökalp still expresses the feelings of the ordinary orthodox Muslim, but they also contain the first signs of a rationalistic and sociological explanation of religious observances. The *zekât* is to be given because "the poor have a right to the possessions of the rich." The profits a man makes are not his private property but belong to the people, whose collective work enables the individual to amass wealth.

Together with this rationalistic approach Gökalp's religious poems have a distinct mystical flavour, the result of the influence of Ṣūfism, which played such a notable part in the development of Turkish Islam. His famous poem *Din* [1] opens with the words:

> My religion is based neither on hope nor on fear,
> I worship my God because I love Him.

Farther on Gökalp addresses the preacher saying:

> Preacher, explain to me divine love.
> I do not care what devil is and what angel.
> Speak of the mystery of the Saints,
> Who is the lover, who the beloved, what is love?

Gökalp tries to revive the popular mystical poetry, the old master of which, Yunus Emre, is regarded by the Turks to-day as one of their great poets. Fischer [2] thinks that Gökalp wanted to renew the custom of children singing such poems in schools. Gökalp himself composed a number of *ilâhiler*, religious poems opening with an address to God and written in simple and straight-forward language:

> Neither far am I (from You) nor near,
> I am disheartened and bewildered.
> I cannot part company, so used am I (to You),
> Let us be friends again, my God. [3]

There are in his religious poems also hints of an idea which he

---

[1] Published in January 1915 in I.M., II, p. 552, and later in Y.H., p. 7.
[2] P. 58, *n.* 77.　　　　　　　　　　[3] Y.H., p. 36.

develops in his theoretical articles, namely that God is but a symbol for the ideal.

> The lover cries for his beloved,
> The soldier dies for his country.
> The student strives for knowledge,
> The aim of all is You, great God.[1]

What Gökalp regards as his highest ideal is shown in the poem *Hayat Yolunda*,[2] which is one of his most revealing poems:

> Whilst I was looking for the Beloved up in heaven,
> I did not find Him there but on earth, in Turan.[3]

In Gökalp's opinion all religion is only a symbolic expression of life. In this way he tries—following Durkheim—to give a rationalistic explanation for the religious ceremonies of Islam. In the concepts of profane and holy he sees a symbol of the contrast between individuality and personality.[4] The "negative" regulations such as fasting, ablution, prohibition of alcohol, the wearing of white garments on the pilgrimage and so forth are intended to free the faithful from his carnal desires which are his individualistic, that is, his animal nature. On the other hand, Islam attempts through its "positive" ceremonies such as prayer, pilgrimage to Mecca, etc., all of which are carried out collectively, to strengthen the personality of the individual in which, as shown above, collective consciousness is reflected.[5] Gökalp advocates a gradual discarding of these symbols, as they only exist because humanity has not yet reached its highest stage of development.

Gökalp tries to solve the contradiction between his mystical and rationalistic trends—the fundamental contradiction in his mind—by an adaptation of Comte's *loi des trois états*. Comte's theory, based on ideas already found in the writings of Saint Simon and Turgot, divides the development of humanity into three stages—the theological (fetishism, polytheism, monotheism), the

---

[1] Y.H., p. 37.    [2] K.E., pp. 88–9.
[3] For Gökalp's belief in Turanism, the ideal of the political or cultural unification of all Turks, see pp. 126–30, *post*.
[4] Regarding these terms, see p. 53, *ante*.    [5] Y.M., 8, p. 146b.

metaphysical (representing an attempt to discover the essence of phenomena through the process of reason), and the positive or scientific. In Gökalp's view, humanity is in the first stage dominated by religion, the faith of the prophets and saints. Later, in the second stage, the doctors of law become the spiritual leaders, and the religious traditions (*nakliyat*) clash with reason and philosophy (*akliyat*). Finally, positive science bridges the gulf between them by showing that tradition is not a rigid dogma but a living expression of historical development which human reason follows. Religion and philosophy show the way to the same goal, the union of the soul with God.[1]

While in his Constantinople period the "holy enthusiasm" (*vecid*) occupies the central position in Gökalp's religious views, in the last years of his life, and particularly after his exile in Malta, he stresses the importance of the more sober concept of reliance on God (*tevekkül*). In this period he strongly emphasizes the importance of Islam as a moral factor and attaches particular value to the religious education of youth. "The people who in all periods of life show strong character," he writes in 1922,[2] "are mostly those who in their youth received a religious education."

## CANON LAW

To support his conception of Islam as a purely ethical religion, free from all legal and social rules, Gökalp develops a new theory of the Islamic canon law (*şeriat*). He distinguishes between two sources of the *şeriat*: (*a*) *nas*,[3] the divine revelation which is transmitted by the Qur'ān and the Sunna (the deeds, utterances and unspoken approval of Muḥammad) and which is absolute and not subject to any alteration; and (*b*) *örf*,[4] in which, as we have

---

[1] See the poem *Dinle Ilim* (Y.H., p. 8).
[2] K.M., 5.      [3] In Arabic *naṣṣ*.
[4] The term *örf* (in Arabic *'urf*) is commonly used in Islamic jurisprudence in the sense of customary or unwritten law laid down by the local and secular authorities (as opposed to canon law). For the particular meaning in which he uses this term Gökalp claims to have found a warrant in the well-known sentence of the Qur'ān: *ta'murūna bi-'l-ma'rūfi wa-tanhauna 'ani 'l-munkari*, "Order the

seen above, the collective consciousness of society, in this case of the Muslim community, is embodied. Like every custom, the Islamic *örf* is modified with the changes in the social structure. Without knowing or at least without mentioning the researches of European orientalists in the field of criticism of the Ḥadīth (the sacred traditions of the Prophet and his companions), Gökalp points out that such modification was already apparent in the first decades of Islam. As a typical example he cites the case of the veil. The covering of the face with a veil was in the beginning an indication of the high social standing of the Muslim woman. The Caliph 'Umar therefore forbade the women servants to wear the veil, which was regarded as the dress of the freeborn. When, however, after the Umayyad period, the influence of non-Arab peoples increased in Islam and all Muslims were recognized as equals, a change occurred also in this customary law and, Gökalp adds, the women servants were allowed to cover their faces with veils. In the course of time the veil became a religious obligation for every Muslim woman, although again for social and economic reasons village women went unveiled.

Since the beginnings of Islam, Gökalp says, Muslim jurists have used the *örf* to explain the law of the Qur'ān and the Sunna and to modify it according to the requirements of the age. The Imām Mālik extended the range of the Sunna, including in it, in addition to the "Way" of the Prophet and his Companions, customs of the inhabitants of Medina. Abū Ḥanīfa introduced the rule of *istiḥsān* (the requirements of the community), which to Gökalp means establishing *örf* as an independent basis besides the four accepted foundations of canon law: Qur'ān, Sunna, Ijmā' (consensus of the community) and Qiyās (analogy).[1] Furthermore, early Muslim

equitable (*maruf* from the same root as *örf*) and abstain from the bad (*münker*)" (Qur'ān, III, 110; see also VII, 199). Gökalp holds, without any proof save certain verbal similarities, that *maruf* and *münker* are what the *örf*, the social consciousness, praises or blames, whereas the equivalent terms in the *nas* are *vacip* and *haram*.

[1] Although Gökalp here erroneously identifies *istiḥsān* with *örf*, he is correct in so far as in the first centuries of Islam there were jurists who recognized

scholars had already laid down that in certain cases *örf* can replace the *nas*, as the Ḥadīth says, "What the faithful regard as good, is good with God." [1] A jurist at the time of Hārūn al-Rashīd, is quoted by Gökalp for the surprising opinion that in the case of contradiction between *örf* and *nas* the former is to be accepted if the *nas* was derived from it.

Gökalp accepts this ruling and expands its scope by affirming that almost all obligations of *nas* which refer to matters of this world have in fact been derived from *örf*, and that even the obligations based only on *nas* have, in order to be applied in practice, to be harmonized with the *örf*. While thus rendering possible radical reforms in the law of Islam, he virtually abandons his previous standpoint that *nas* is the divine law, unchangeable and everlasting. In this way he reaches the conclusion that with the exception of the personal relationship between man and God all religious obligations depend for their sanction on the "social consciousness". Gökalp finds a basis for this view in the divine words, "So spake God: where the law does not conform to the *örf*, change the law and make it conform to the *örf*." [2] The theory of social consciousness as the major factor in the development of the canon law of Islam will, in Gökalp's opinion, not undermine the religious sentiment of the Muslim. Gökalp regards *örf*, or at least the law working in it, as a divine revelation. Just as some Muslim theologians hold that God reveals himself in the laws of nature, so it should be permissible to regard the law determining social life as divine.

For further research into the Islamic *örf* and its development Gökalp advocates the establishment of a new branch of science

*örf* as the fifth fundamental principle of law. Despite the important rôle *örf* played de facto in the legal life of all Muslim peoples, it was never fully recognized by official jurisprudence (see I. Goldziher, *Die Zāhiriten* (Leipzig, 1884), pp. 204–6; *Encycl. of Islām*, IV, pp. 323–4, 1031).

[1] A highly arbitrary interpretation of the Ḥadīth *mā ra'aha 'l-mu'minūna ḥasanan fa-huwa 'inda 'llāhi 'l-ḥasanu.*

[2] The source of these words is not quoted. In general, Gökalp's references to Islamic traditions in support of his theories have to be accepted with much caution.

which he calls the "science of the social roots of the law" (*içtimaî usul-ü fıkıh*). While the traditional *usul-ü fıkıh* explores how the obligations of Islam are based on *nas*, the new science—in which theologians will co-operate with sociologists—will deal with the development of *örf* in the different Muslim societies and with the changes it has brought about in canon law.[1]

## SEPARATION OF RELIGION AND STATE

On the basis of his daring theory of canon law, Gökalp is able to suggest far-reaching religious reforms. His main aims are two: (*a*) to separate religion and State, that is, to put an end to the domination of Islam over the political and social life of the Turkish nation, and (*b*) to separate religion and Oriental civilization and thus make possible the maintenance of the fundamental values of Islam side by side with European civilization and Turkish national culture.

Gökalp believes that the harmful intermingling of religious institutions with the State goes back to early Islam. Since the pagan Arabs lacked an organized form of government, institutions of the religious community and of the young Muslim State had to be established at the same time and made interdependent. Had the foreign kings whom Muḥammad is said to have invited to embrace Islam adopted the new religion, the political and religious organizations of the Muslims might have developed separately and therefore, in Gökalp's opinion, in a more satisfactory way. During the first generations of Islam the *ulema* (clergy) were not given any official status. They did not play any active part in Government, and the rulers, on the other hand, did not interfere with their work. However, after a short time the *ulema* were integrated into the administration of the State. Thus they lost their ecclesiastical

I.M., 2., pp. 40–44; 3, pp. 84–7; Y.M., 9, p. 166b; 38, pp. 244c–225a; Y.H., p. 28. H. A. R. Gibb regards Gökalp's theory of *nas* and *örf* as "purely subjective" and "irreconcilable with the bases of Islamic thought" (*Modern Trends in Islam* (Chicago, 1947), p. 92).

independence but gained an increasing influence on the Government. This state of affairs existed in the Ottoman Empire until the beginning of this century.[1]

Now the time has come, Gökalp maintains, to separate the spheres of activity of the secular and religious authorities. All remnants of theocracy and clericalism must be eliminated from political life and full internal sovereignty must be secured for the State. The legislative powers of the nation should not be limited by canon law. There can be no strong and independent State "which does not make its laws itself, but regards them as sent from heaven and as unchangeable."[2] Although this principle is in obvious contradiction to the essence of Islam, Gökalp claims support for it from the Qur'ān which says, "Obey the word of God and the word of the Prophet and those in authority among you."[3] Gökalp comments: "In matters of belief and worship the Qur'ān and Sunna decide, and in case of doubt the Muslim has to ask for the advice of the Mufti. But legislation is the function of the secular authorities (*ululemir*), i.e. the State."[4]

This conception leads Gökalp to demand radical changes in the structure of the State. First of all, in the future secular State, there will be no more room for the traditional office of the *Şeyhülislâm*, who not only was the highest authority on religious matters, the head of the *ulema* and the supreme Mufti, but who, as an important member of the Cabinet, also used to examine whether the laws of the State conformed to canon law. Gökalp demands the transfer of his legal authority (*kaza*) to the State. His right to give decisions (*ifta*) should be limited to questions of belief and religious ceremonies. The *Şeyhülislâm*, like every

---

[1] Y.M., 57, pp. 82c–83a; 67, p. 2a.

[2] See the poem *Meşihat* (quoted in Fischer, p. 62). This poem was censored by the Young Turk Government which did not dare openly to challenge the traditional conception of the Muslim State.

[3] *Aṭīʿū 'llāha wa-aṭīʿū 'r-rasūla wa-ūlī 'l-amri minkum* (Qur'ān, IV, 59). This verse had already been quoted with a similar intention by Mansurizade M. Sait in 1914 (I.M., I, p. 281).  [4] Y.H., p. 28.

other Mufti, should be a scholar and independent of the political authorities.[1]

On this important question Gökalp was not satisfied, as he usually was, with making suggestions but he tried to carry them out in practice. In 1917 he submitted to the Congress of the Union and Progress Party a detailed memorandum based on historical, sociological and legal researches, in which he demanded the virtual abolition of the office of the *Şeyhülislâm* in its traditional form.[2] The party leaders accepted his views, after the Government had, in 1916–17, already decided to transfer the administration of the religious courts to the Ministry of Justice and the supervision of the religious schools to the Ministry of Education. Most of these reforms of the Young Turk Government were cancelled after the 1918 armistice. Several years later, however, Atatürk abolished the office of the *Şeyhülislâm* and transferred the remnants of his functions to a Government department for religious affairs (*Diyanet İşleri Reisliği*).

In the same memorandum Gökalp called for the abolition of another religious institution which was of paramount importance to the economic and legal life of the country, the Ministry of Pious Foundations. The system of endowments (*evkaf*, Arabic *waqf*), in which "the reins of power are given into the hands of the dead", had, Gökalp maintained, done considerable harm to the Turkish nation. Every Waqf was a kind of *imperium in imperio* with its own constitution, officials and budget. The existence of these endowments prevented the establishment of a central communal administration in the towns, since many schools, hospitals, water reservoirs, public wells, etc., were the property of religious organizations, either Muslim or Christian. Particularly in Constantinople there had been continuous friction between the Municipality (*Şehir Emaneti*), the Ministry of Pious Foundations and the Christian Patriarchates. This prevented all progressive

---

[1] Y.H., p. 28; E., p. 161; and the poems *Meşihat* and *Halife ve Müfti* in Y.H.
[2] See the memoirs of Muhittin Birgen, former editor of the *Tanin* (A.I., pp. 8–10).

economic planning by the local authorities and the State. The Waqf system had also a detrimental effect on the character of the Turkish people. The so-called private Waqf which secured for the descendants of the founder an income without work fostered in the people what Gökalp calls the typical faults of dervishes, the exaggerated reliance on God and the blind belief in fate, which sapped the initiative of the Turkish masses and bred indolence. Gökalp holds that true Islam is opposed to fatalism and requires everybody to examine the nature of social facts and their reasons (*içtihat*) and to work for improvement and progress (*mücadele*).[1] This is the main reason for his opposition to the dervish orders, although they played a very important rôle in the development of Turkish culture, which in all its other aspects is so very dear to Gökalp.

There was no remedy but to transfer the administration of the "genuine Waqf" (*evkaf-ı mazbute*) to the local authorities—that is, in the villages to the District Councils and in the towns to the Municipalities. With regard to the *evkaf-ı mülhaka*, which are subject only to the supervision of the Ministry of Pious Foundations, he suggested that they should remain under the control of their administrators (*mütevelli*) and the local authorities should only supervise them.[2]

Gökalp's demand was partly fulfilled some months before his death. In March 1924 the Ministry of Pious Foundations was abolished and instead a General Waqf Administration was established under the supervision of the Prime Minister.[3] In 1930 many endowments were transferred to the local authorities without, however, abrogating the Waqf system entirely.

In the field of academic education too Gökalp wanted to put an end to the dualism of secular and religious systems. The main religious colleges (*medrese*) should be merged with the Theological

[1] Y.M., 56, pp. 62c–63a.
[2] Y.H., pp. 29, 30; K.M., 33.
[3] For the text of the law, see A. J. Toynbee, *Survey of Internat. Affairs*, 1925, I, pp. 572–4.

Faculty of the Constantinople University (*darülfünun*).[1] Atatürk followed Gökalp's advice and abolished the *medrese*,[2] but the Theological Faculty too was closed in 1933.

### CALIPHATE

The principal institution affected by Gökalp's theory of separation between religious and political life was the Ottoman monarchy which united the position of a secular ruler (Sultan) with the office of the head of the Muslim community (Caliph). Had Gökalp been completely consistent, he should have demanded the abolition of this institution from the outset. In the period of Young Turk rule, however, he did not dare to do so openly, but tried to modify its powers without changing its name. In a poem written during the First World War [3] Gökalp describes the Caliph as the highest law-making authority, who relies on *örf* and *ijmā'* and whose advisory council is Parliament. After the Caliph's prestige had declined in consequence of his opposition to the national movement of Atatürk, Gökalp went a step further. In the *Foundations of Turkism* he demands the abolition of all theocratic rule, defined as "law-making by Caliphs and Sultans who are regarded as God's shadow upon earth".[4] Atatürk's revolution which separated the Sultanate from the Caliphate met with his full approval. In November 1922, the Great National Assembly in Ankara abolished the Sultanate. Vahidettin remained only Caliph and after his flight Abdul Mejid was elected by the Assembly to replace him.

Gökalp now saw an opportunity of reorganizing the religious institutions on a new basis, more or less on the lines of the Christian Churches of the West. He envisages an "Islamic Church" of which the basic unit would be the community (*cemaat*) defined as the "local assembly of the faithful who meet to worship under the leadership of the Imam". The smallest place

---

[1] Y.H., p. 32.

[2] See "Law for the Unification of Educational Systems" of March 1924, quoted in A. J. Toynbee, loc. cit.

[3] *Halife ve Müfti*, published in Y.H.    [4] E., p. 161.

of worship, the "parish" mosque (*mahalle mescidi*), is linked with the larger mosque (*cami*), and the latter with the main mosque of the town (*cami-i kebir*), the head of which is a Mufti. All the Muftis of the country would be subject to the authority of the Mufti of the capital who would bear the traditional title of Şeyhülislâm. He and his colleagues in the other Muslim countries would owe allegiance to the Caliph, the head of the international Islamic community or "Church" (*ümmet*), whose position would be, in some respects, similar to that of the Pope in the Catholic Church. The Caliph would convene religious assemblies in which representatives of all the Muslim nations would take part, such as conferences of Muftis and congresses to deal with religious education, improvement of theological studies, etc.[1] The idea of such Islamic congresses was not new, Gökalp had suggested it some ten years before in *Türk Yurdu*.[2] But in those days he had tried to lay down for the Muslim *ümmet* a number of principles which he does not mention later: the use of Arab characters in all Muslim languages, the creation of a uniform scientific terminology, the introduction of a common calendar (solar year but counting from the Hijra),[3] etc. Gökalp expresses the hope that the organization of the *ümmet* on these lines would bring about a general revival of religious life and would restore to Islam the splendour it had enjoyed in the time of the Prophet.[4]

Gökalp's plan was not carried out. The idea of turning the Caliphate into a purely spiritual authority was incompatible with the fundamental conceptions of Islam and did not appeal to the Turkish people. Furthermore, Atatürk and his friends feared that the Caliphate would remain the rallying point of all those forces, both in Turkey and other parts of the Muslim world, which were

---

[1] Y.M., 67, p. 2b; see also the article *Türk Harsı ve Osmanlı Medeniyeti* in the paper *Hakimiyet-i Milliye* of 16 May 1923 (quoted in Deny, p. 16).

[2] T., p. 33.

[3] This point had already been dropped in the second version of his article which appeared in 1918 in T., because a short while earlier the Young Turk Government had introduced another calendar.

[4] Y.M., 67, p. 2b.

opposed to the radical secularization of the new Turkish State. In March, 1924, a few months before Gökalp's death, the Caliphate was abolished by act of the Turkish Parliament. In 1928 Islam lost even its position as the official religion of the State, and in 1937 a sentence was inserted in Clause 2 of the Turkish Constitution defining the character of the State, inter alia, as "secular" (*lâik*). The separation of religion and State was complete.

### REFORM OF FAMILY LAW

In another sphere Gökalp's demand for the abolition of canon law met with much success. He regards a reform in the position of the Turkish woman as one of the most urgent necessities for the progress of his people. The moral crisis and the loosening of family ties which resulted from the First World War increased his interest in the question. Surveying the position of women in the past, he describes with enthusiasm her high status in ancient Turkish society. Islam put woman on an equal footing with men in the matter of sexual morality. But its attitude towards women's legal rights was determined by the conditions of Arab society in the days of Muḥammad, when equality of the sexes was unheard of. Thus Islamic law gives the husband an easy right to divorce, while at the same time regarding it, from a moral point of view, as "a most odious concession". The right of marrying more than one wife, too, carried with it the requirement that the husband should treat all his wives with "equity", a condition which in practice ought to prevent a conscientious Muslim from making use of this right. In early Islam women had a high social standing which, however, under Persian and Byzantine influence greatly deteriorated. The obligation to cover the face with a veil and the seclusion of women in the harem were foreign customs which were accepted in Islamic society and became religious obligations at least in the towns.[1]

[1] Y.M., 9, pp. 166b–168a; 14, pp. 261a–265b; 15, pp. 281a–285a; E., p. 155. Gökalp's teacher Durkheim, too, although living under the totally different social conditions of France, demanded greater co-operation of women in public life (*Suicide*, pp. 442–4).

Gökalp strongly objects to this discrimination against women. How can it be, he asks, that women, who as mothers, sisters, wives, or daughters evoke the most sacred feelings in our hearts, are regarded by the law as inferior creatures? "Certainly the commentators (of the Qur'ān) have made a mistake." [1] The woman is the centre of the family on which the State is based, and without her co-operation social life is defective. In many of his poems Gökalp praises the Turkish woman and particularly the rôle she played during Atatürk's war of independence, when she did man's work at home and in the field, attended to the wounded and moved munitions to the front at the risk of her life. "The new life will begin ", wrote Gökalp to his daughter from his exile in Malta [2], "when women have the same education as men and are allowed to occupy leading positions in public life." Therefore it is vital to abrogate the canon law of Islam which grants the man superior rights with regard to marriage, divorce and inheritance. Full political rights too must be given to Turkish women, and they should be allowed to enter schools and universities without any discrimination. The prejudice against a woman's earning her own living must be entirely given up. Gökalp was confirmed in his views by the social changes which took place during and after the First World War, when many Turkish women were employed in public services and others entered professions hitherto regarded as the exclusive domain of men. He also welcomed the transition from the large patriarchal family residing in a big *konak* (mansion) to the small monogamic family in the *yuva* (literally, nest). [3]

Under the Young Turk régime, however, he had not the courage to press openly for radical reforms of family law. According to one of his colleagues, [4] Gökalp attacked the veiling and seclusion

---

[1] Y.H., p. 27.

[2] Ali Nüzhet, p. 102.

[3] Y.H., pp. 17, 18, 25–6, 27; Fahri, p. 230; K.M., 21; E., p. 162. A fuller account of Gökalp's views on the position of women and family law is given in the book of Ziyaeddin Fahri who regards Gökalp's treatment of these questions as one of the most important parts of his work.

[4] Ahmed Emin, p. 234.

of women in a pamphlet which he printed on a copying machine and circulated privately. In this publication he declared that veiling was a social usage which could be traced to certain primitive instincts and ancient social institutions and that its perpetuation in the present century was the greatest possible insult to Turkish women.

The 1917 Family Law, in the preparation of which Gökalp took a leading part, fulfilled a portion of his requirements. Under this law marriage was no longer regarded as a purely religious affair. While polygamy was not entirely prohibited, women were granted the right of stipulating monogamy by a special clause in their contract of marriage. Gökalp's suggestions were fully carried out only by Atatürk. In 1926 Turkey adopted a new civil code based on the Swiss law. (In fact, it is a translation of the Swiss *Code Civil* and does not attempt to incorporate Turkish national traditions which, in Gökalp's opinion, should serve as a basis for all legal regulations.) Polygamy became illegal, divorce was made more difficult, and women were given equal rights with men in the matter of inheritance.[1] A few years later the Turkish woman obtained both the right to vote and the right to stand for election. The percentage of girls in all educational institutions grew yearly, the principle of co-education was introduced in colleges and universities, and women began to enter all the professions.

In the modern Turkish Republic another of Gökalp's ideas with regard to family law was adopted, the demand that every Turk should have a proper family name.[2] In July 1934, a decree was issued requiring every citizen of the Republic to choose a family name within a definite period. Until then the Muslim Turks had borne mostly Arabic or Persian names, many of them of religious significance. Owing to the growing interest in Turkish antiquity —largely a result of Gökalp's work [3]—many people chose old

---

[1] See Count Léon Ostrorog, *The Angora Reform* (London, 1927), pp. 87–93.
[2] Fahri, pp. 147–8. See Gökalp's article *Türklerde Aile Adları* (Family Names among the Turks) in K.M., 33.
[3] See pp. 112–15 below.

Turkish names as their family names. Exactly as at the turn of the nineteenth century Greek ships began to bear the names of heroes of pagan antiquity instead of those of saints of the Church, so many pre-Islamic Turkish names were revived. Gökalp's own pen-name is an early example of the existence of this trend in Turkish nationalist circles. In recent years Turkish names have begun to supersede even the traditional Islamic given names.

### ISLAM AND MODERN CIVILIZATION

Just as Gökalp demands the separation of Church and State, so, in his view, religion and civilization ought to be kept separate. As mentioned above, he disapproves of the term "Islamic civilization", since he regards the civilization which had developed in the Muslim countries of Western Asia as the continuation of the Byzantine and Persian civilizations. Gökalp holds that religion in its proper sense of the totality of beliefs and ceremonies is not bound to any specific civilization. Islam, therefore, could be combined with modern European civilization just as well as it had merged in the past with Oriental civilization. Gökalp denies any conflict between science and religion generally, and particularly in Islam which always set reason on a higher plane than other religions did. Such contradiction exists only in the opinion of narrow-minded clergymen (*hoca*) who regard every scientific truth as an unorthodox innovation (*bid'at*). By their fanaticism these religious teachers have estranged the Turkish intelligentsia from Islam and at the same time have neglected to combat the illiteracy of the masses.[1]

This view on Islam and modern civilization represents a certain advance over Gökalp's original theories. At first he considers that the Turks participate in an international Islamic civilization. Later, however, he reaches the conclusion that in the modern world civilization is no longer based on a community of religion,

[1] T., pp. 8–9, 35–6; Y.M., 27, p. 2a–b; 29, p. 42a–b; K.E., p. 123; Y.H., p. 8; E., pp. 50–54.

6

as is proved by the entry of non-Christian nations into the circle
of Western civilization.[1] The foundations of modern European
civilization are the positive sciences, and these render it equally
accessible to the Turkish nation. It is significant that in an article
which was originally published in the beginning of 1914 [2] Gökalp
still speaks of *İslâm beynelmilliyeti*, the Islamic International,
expressing itself in its own civilization. In the text of the same
article as published some four years later,[3] he changed this term
to *İslâm ümmetçiliği*, relegating Islam to the status of a religious
community. By adopting this view he seriously diminished the
importance of Islam as a cultural factor, though at the time he did
not admit this. Henceforth, Gökalp in practice no longer recognized Islam as an independent spiritual force in the life of his
people, but acknowledged religious values only in so far as they
were absorbed in Turkish national culture.

### ISLAM AND TURKISH NATIONALISM

Modern Islam, as Gökalp understands it, can easily be combined
with Turkish nationalism and national culture. He rejects the
opinion of Muslim orthodoxy which holds that Islam and the
idea of nationalism are fundamentally contradictory. In his usual
way he finds support for his view in the Qur'ān, which says:
"And we have made you peoples and tribes so that you should
know each other."[4] With an arbitrariness worthy of an ancient
commentator Gökalp explains that "to know each other" means
to know each other's language, and the verse refers therefore
to people speaking the same language, that is, nations. For
additional support Gökalp quotes the Qur'ān verse "And to
every nation (We have sent) a guide" [5] and a passage from the
Ḥadīth. From all this he concludes that Islam advocates modern

[1] T., pp. 8–10; E., pp. 78–9.
[2] I.M., 1, p. 15 (*İslâm Terbiyesinin Mahiyeti*).
[3] T., p. 36 (under the heading *Terbiye*).
[4] *Wa-ja'alnākum shu'ūban wa-qabā'ila li-ta'ārafū* (XLIX, 13).
[5] *Wa-li-kulli qawmin hādin* (XIII, 7).

nationalism which aims at establishing States composed of single, homogeneous nations.[1]

In his early years Gökalp used to stress the importance of Islam for strengthening Turkish patriotism. Those were the years of the struggle of the Ottoman Empire against its Christian enemies outside and inside its borders: the Tripoli war against Italy, the 1912–13 wars against the Christian countries in the Balkans, the Armenian disturbances in Anatolia and the beginning of the First World War. During this period *Jihād*, the Holy War against the unbelievers, was an excellent battle-cry for rousing and uniting the Turkish masses. Gökalp wrote many patriotic poems in this spirit, one of which, the "Prayer of a Soldier", runs as follows:

> My heart's desires are two: religion and Fatherland . . .
> Our way is the Holy War, its end martyrdom. . . .
> Have mercy on Islam, take revenge on its enemies,
> Make Islam flourish, O God.[2]

In the "Chant (*ilâhi*) for Children", which is imbued with a strong hatred of the Bulgarians with whom the Turks were then at war, he says:

> The Crescent shall not submit to the Cross—Amen.
> It shall not be said: the Turks are lost—Amen. . . .
> Give us a religion of light, a faith of fire,
> Let us bring back to Islam the people who have strayed
>     from its path.[3]

The "conscience of Europe", writes Gökalp bitterly during the Balkan wars, is nothing but a name for the concert of Christian nations; international co-operation in Europe is limited to those countries. As a counterpart to this, Gökalp at that period stressed the spiritual kinship of the Muslim nations. In the national calamity of the Tripoli and Balkan wars moral support came to the Turks not from those akin to them racially or linguistically like

---

[1] T., pp. 61–2; Y.M., 67, p. 2a.
[2] K.E., p. 83.
[3] K.E., pp. 81–2; see also the poems in K.E., pp. 94, 98, 125–7.

the Hungarians and Mongolians, but from the Muslims even in countries as distant as India, Java and China.[1]

Gökalp finds an explanation for this combination of Turkish patriotism with Islamic feeling in the fact that unlike Albanians and Egyptians *all* the Turks are Muslims and their political capital is their religious centre. He expressly defines the Turkish nation as the totality of Turkish-speaking Muslims. In his opinion Turkey is the last fortress of Islam, and with the national renaissance of the Turks a period of Muslim religious revival will begin.[2]

This emphasis on religious feeling as a basis of Turkish patriotism is found in Gökalp's writings until the beginning of the First World War. In the poem *Kızıl Destan*, which describes the outbreak of the war from a narrowly Turkish standpoint, he tries to find the causes of the international conflict in the occupation of Muslim countries by Western Powers.[3] But the Albanian revolt, the failure of the declaration of the Holy War by the Ottoman Government, the participation of Indian and other Muslim troops in the war on the side of Turkey's enemies, and finally the Arab revolt against the Sultan largely softened the Islamic note in Gökalp's writings. In the same measure his conviction that the Turks were a European nation and had to accept Western civilization became stronger during the war years. However, all these events did not entirely destroy his Islamic patriotism. These feelings again found strong expression when the Turks were involved in another grim war against Christian enemies, this time against the Greeks supported by the British in the West, the Armenians in the East and the French in the South-East (1919–22). *Kolsuz Hanım*, an allegorical poem written in those days, describes how the Turks had in the past defended Islam against the unbelievers.[4] In a historical play, also published in the summer of 1922, Gökalp revives the memory of the Seljuq ruler Alp Arslan, the defender of the faith, and contrasts the tolerance of Islam with

---

[1] T., p. 8.
[2] T., pp. 31, 34; Y.M., 43, p. 322b; 51, p. 482b.
[3] K.E., pp. 128–32.
[4] K.M., 5.

the savagery of Christianity.[1] The peace treaty of Sèvres (1920) and the establishment of Western mandatory rule in a number of Muslim countries proves to Gökalp that the fanatical mentality of the Crusaders has not yet passed away in Europe.[2]

Gökalp's Islamic patriotism, however, never led him to embrace Pan-Islamism as a political creed. The idea of uniting all Muslim nations under one ruler is in Gökalp's opinion merely a messianic hope. In our times every Muslim nation has the duty of fighting for its own liberation from foreign rule and for social progress. The Pan-Islamic movement, which under foreign, particularly German, influence had gained considerable strength in the time of Abdul Hamid and the beginning of the Young Turk régime, did not bring any beneficial results. It created a theocratic ideology which stood in the way of national revival and of the establishment of a modern democratic State. Gökalp approves of Pan-Islamic sentiment only as a basis for co-operation between the Muslim nations for the purpose of attaining the objects mentioned. Accordingly, he stresses the importance of a common religion as a political factor unifying the Turks and Arabs in the Ottoman Empire and linking the Muslims in Turkey with their Turkish co-religionists in Russia. In both cases he seeks to use the religious ties for strengthening the Turkish nation, the interests of which are always dearer to him than those of Islam.[3]

## A NATIONAL RELIGION?

Gökalp occasionally hints at the necessity of giving Islam a national Turkish character. In his Turanist period, that is in the years preceding the outbreak of the First World War, he regretfully points out that Islam, or at least a considerable part of its institutions, has originated from the culture of foreign peoples. "We have accepted the religions of the Arabs, the Persians and

---

[1] K.M., 3.
[2] E., pp. 78–9.
[3] T., pp. 34, 60–63; Y.M., 35, p. 163b–c; 37, p. 202a–b; 38, p. 234b; Y.H. (quoted in Deny, pp. 20–21); E., pp. 11, 75.

the Europeans," says the Turkish sage in the poem *Kızıl Elma* reproachfully,[1] following Herder who "felt deeply for all those many primitive peoples who had lost the religion of their ancestors, and with it, their character, their heart, and their history." [2] The Turkish scholars have to find out which are the genuine beliefs and traditions of Islam and which are local customs or later innovations that Islam has absorbed from the Arabs, the Persians, and from other nations.[3] The latter, Gökalp seems to think without saying so explicitly, should be discarded as foreign elements which are not consistent with the Turkish national spirit. The inclusion of Arab traditions among the non-essential parts of Islam provides a theoretical basis for an almost boundless "purification" of Muslim religion.

Except, however, for these vague demands for the elimination of foreign elements in Islam, Gökalp has very little to offer in the way of practical suggestions. His one positive contribution is the demand, which had also been made by Herder,[4] that religious worship should be conducted in the language of the people, i.e. in Turkish instead of Arabic. He asserts that the most popular ceremonies in Turkey are those which have always been carried out in the Turkish language, such as the *münacat*, the private prayers which are said after the obligatory prayer (*namaz*); the *ilâhiler* (chants), particularly those recited in the nights of Ramaḍān; the *mevlûd-ü şerif*, the popular story of the birth of the Prophet, recited in memory of the dead and on other occasions; the songs used in the *zikir* exercises of the dervishes, and others. Gökalp demands that the call to prayer (*ezan*), the sermons (*hutbe*, *vaız*) and the general prayers (*dua*), that is, the whole liturgy with the exception of the fixed Qur'ān recitation (*tilâvet*) should be recited in the national tongue. In support of his demand

---

[1] K.E., p. 23. Gökalp regards, for instance, the "ascetic" trend in Islam as an Arab element which is uncongenial to the Turks.

[2] H. Kohn, *Idea of Nationalism*, p. 449.

[3] T., p. 37.

[4] See H. Kohn, ibid.

Gökalp cites the Imam Abū Ḥanīfa, the founder of the legal school prevailing in Turkey, who allowed prayers in every language. The Qur'ān should be taught in schools in the Turkish translation, which would help to spread knowledge and love of religion among the masses of the people.[1]

This was the line taken by the *İslâm Mecmuası*, on the editorial board of which Gökalp played a leading part. The issues of this periodical opened with Qur'ānic verses translated into Turkish, a practice prohibited by orthodox Islam. After Gökalp's death his disciples tried to carry out his proposals. The Theological Faculty of the Constantinople University appointed a committee to enquire into the possibility of a scientific reform of Islam. Köprülüzade Fuat, the Turcologist and follower of Gökalp, served as chairman of this committee which in the summer of 1928 submitted its report to the Ministry of Education.[2] The chief suggestion made by the report, which clearly shows the influence of Gökalp's theories, was to improve the service in the mosques through the introduction of the Turkish language in prayers, sermons and readings from the Qur'ān, as well as by the use of musical instruments and by making the sermons more thoughtful and varied. The Government did not accept even these moderate reforms and dissolved the committee. When the Istanbul University was reorganized in 1933 the Government abolished the Theological Faculty, establishing an Institute for Islamic Research in its place. In modern Turkey the call to prayer in Arabic as well as the study of the Qur'ān (both in the original and the Turkish translation) in schools, and, in fact, all religious education have been forbidden. Atatürk and his collaborators were convinced that Islam and Turkish nationalism were incompatible. In recent years, however, a certain modification of this anti-Islamic policy has been discernible.[3]

---

[1] Y.H., p. 9; E., pp. 163–4; see also Şapolyo, pp. 162–3.

[2] See L. Levonian, *The Turkish Press*, 1925–32 (Athens, 1932), pp. 123–6.

[3] See U. Heydt, *Islam in Modern Turkey* (in *Royal Central Asian Journal*, London, July–October, 1947, pp. 299–308).

# V

# TURKISM

## THE TURKIST MOVEMENT

In Gökalp's opinion national movements, at any rate among Oriental peoples, pass through three stages. They begin with a cultural awakening; they then assume the form of a political movement; and finally they also formulate an economic programme.[1] In accordance with this view Gökalp endeavours to find the roots of modern Turkish nationalism in an intellectual and cultural movement which he calls Turkism (*Türkçülük*).[2]

In his analysis of the rise of Turkism [3] Gökalp specifies a number of causes, some of them positive, others negative. Among the latter he emphasizes particularly the decay of the traditional values which took place in Islamic-Turkish society. The political and cultural decline of the Muslim countries in general, and of the Ottoman Empire in particular, in contrast with the progress of the West, awakened in the mind of the educated Turk a desire for a new ideology. The idea of nationalism which began to penetrate from Europe to the East showed him the path to follow. At first, however, the new ideals brought only harm to the Turks. The Christians, and after them the non-Turkish Muslims (e.g. Albanians and Arabs) in the Ottoman Empire, took up the cry of nationalism with enthusiasm and threw off—or tried to throw off—the yoke of Turkish rule. Gökalp indicates, although not

---

[1] E., p. 68.

[2] The use of this term in Gökalp's writings is, however, not confined to this sense. He also speaks of political Turkism, economic Turkism, and so forth. In these cases the term means something like nationalism or national ideal (as opposed to the static term *Türklük* which stands for Turkishness or Turkish nationality).

[3] The following chapter is based solely on Gökalp's own account of the origin of the Turkish national movement.

Western influence, political Turkism was brought into being through the efforts of a number of Turkish intellectuals from Russia. Among the founders of this movement Gökalp mentions İsmail Gasprinski (1841-1914), who produced in the Crimea a paper called *Tercüman*, which had for its motto *Dilde, fikirde, işte birlik* (Unity in Language, Thought and Action) and for its object the cultural and political unification of the Turks.

A more direct influence on the young intelligentsia—Ziya Gökalp among them—was exercised by Hüseyinzade Ali. He was the grandson of a highly esteemed Muslim scholar in the Caucasus who counted among his close friends Ākhūndzāde Fatḥ 'Alī (Mirza Fath Ali Akhundov), author of some Azeri-Turkish comedies which Gökalp read with great enjoyment in his youth. While studying at the University of St. Petersburg, Hüseyinzade was strongly impressed by the two ideas which at that time fired the minds of the Russian students, Socialism and Pan-Slavism. On coming to Constantinople at the beginning of the nineties, he entered the Faculty of Medicine (*Tıbbiye*) and began to disseminate among his fellow-students ideas of social reform and of Pan-Turkism (Turanism). Gökalp relates that one day while Hüseyinzade Ali was sitting in the lecture hall he suddenly called out—just like Archimedes—"I have found it, I have found it." When the others asked what he had found, he answered: "I have found the name of our social malady—*Yangeldizm*" (in the sense of apathy). He meant to say that the cause of the decline of the Turks was that for centuries they had watched the progress of the European nations "with the fatalism of dervishes". Hüzeyinzade's song *Turan*, which preceded Gökalp's poem of the same name, was the first poetical call to Turkish unity. After fighting in the war between Turkey and Greece (1897) he crossed over to Baku in Russian Azerbaijan. There he started a nationalist movement which united the Sunnites and Shiites and worked for the spread of Ottoman-Turkish culture and the strengthening of ties with Turkey.

While still in Constantinople Hüseyinzade was an active

member of the revolutionary society *Osmanlı İttihat ve Terakki Cemiyeti* (Ottoman Society for Union and Progress) which was formed in the *Tıbbiye* on the model of the secret societies in Russia. Among its founders was, as mentioned above, Abdullah Cevdet who after completing his studies worked for some time in Diyarbekir where he strongly influenced the young Gökalp. The name of the society was subsequently transferred to another revolutionary organization (*Hürriyet*), which was founded in European Turkey and brought about the revolution of 1908–9— the Committee of Union and Progress.[1]

Gökalp finds another source of Turkish nationalism in the Pan-Islamic movement. Its herald, the Shaikh Jamāl ud-Dīn al-Afghānī, who called upon the Muslim nations to liberate themselves from the rule of Christian Europe, had numerous disciples in all Islamic countries (e.g. Muḥammad 'Abduh in Egypt, Riya ud-Dīn ibn Fakhr ud-Dīn among the Turks in Russia). He also had a considerable influence on the young nationalists in Constantinople where he spent his last years.[2] In the year of the Shaikh's death (1897), at the time of the Turco-Greek war, his Turkish disciple Mehmet Emin published his well-known national poem which commences with the words *Ben bir Türküm, dinim, cinsimuludur* (I am a Turk, my religion and my race are noble). The poems of Mehmet Emin are written in popular language and in the Turkish "syllabic metre". Like Hüseyinzade, Mehmet Emin linked his nationalism with love for the masses, and especially for the wretched peasants of Antolia.[3]

[1] Y.M., 40, pp. 262a–263b; E., p. 8. On the origin of the Society see the account of one of its founders: İbrahim Temo, *İttihad ve Terakki Cemiyetinin Teşekkülü*, 1939. (Excerpts from this book can be found in Şapolyo, pp. 47–59.) Among the Turkish leaders from Russia who found a refuge in Constantinople and influenced the Turkist movement may be mentioned, in addition to İsmail Gasprinski and Hüseyinzade Ali, two friends of Gökalp, Ağaoğlu Ahmet and Akçoraoğlu Yusuf, the founder of *Türk Yurdu*.

[2] Al-Afghānī "brought inspiration and a popular program to the Pan-Islamic movement by restating the bases of the Islamic community in terms of nationalism" (H.A.R. Gibb, op. cit., p. 27).

[3] Y.M., 40, p. 263a–b; E., p. 9. Akçoraoğlu wrote in 1904 that Mehmet Emin and his associates Şemsettin Sami, Necip Asım, Velet Çelebi and Hasan

The organ of Turkism was for some time the paper *İkdam*, edited by Ahmet Cevdet. The excessive linguistic purism (*tasfiyecilik*) which was affected by this circle, however, alienated the majority of the intellectuals from the paper. The same cause prevented another organ of the movement, *Türk Derneği,* from winning a large circle of readers, especially when as a result of the 1908 revolution Ottomanism became the dominant movement in Turkey.

From the following year, however, Turkism began to make progress. In Salonika the most active spirits in the Turkist movement like Gökalp, Ömer Seyfettin, Ahmet Hikmet and others founded the review *Genç Kalemler* (Young Pens). In Constantinople the periodical *Türk Yurdu* (Turkish Homeland) began to appear and the *Türk Ocağı* Society was founded. Halide Edib published her political novel *Yeni Turan* (New Turan), and Köprülüzade Fuat gave to Turkism a scientific basis through his Turcological researches. From this point the movement continued to grow until it drew into its ranks the majority of the Turkish intellectuals. Among the numerous periodicals representing the views of this movement the principal place was occupied by *Yeni Mecmua* (New Review), which commenced to appear in July 1917, and the policy of which was actually determined by Gökalp. Atatürk's revolution, Gökalp concludes, has realized the aims of the Turkist movement completely.[1]

## THE TURKISH "NATIONAL SPIRIT"

According to Gökalp it was he himself who supplied the theoretical basis for the Turkist movement in his essay *Yeni Hayat ve*

Tahsin were the leaders of a circle, more scientific than political, of intellectuals in Constantinople whose motto was Turkish nationalism. Particularly noteworthy is the opinion of Akçoraoğlu that the founding of this circle was due to German cultural influence and especially to German historiography and philology. The first years of this century were a period of political and economic rapprochement between Constantinople and Berlin.

[1] E., pp. 9–13. This brief sketch of the origins of Turkism by Gökalp is naturally incomplete in many respects. For example, among the European Turcologists who contributed to the rise of Turkism no mention has been made of famous scholars like W. Radloff, H. Vámbéry, I. Kúnos, V. Thomsen, etc.

*Yeni Kıymetler* (New Life and New Values), which was published in 1911 in *Genç Kalemler*.[1] At that time Gökalp sought to make the national revival of the Turkish language, which was the aim of this periodical, a stepping-stone to a similar renaissance in other fields of culture and social life. (At the same time it should be observed that Gökalp never freed himself from the obsession of the special importance of the question of language and its revival.) In contrast to purely literary movements like *Servet-i Fünun* and *Fecr-i Ati*, the object of this movement, which Gökalp at first designated *Yeni Hayat* (New Life), was to pave the way for a social revolution which would complete the political revolution of 1908–9. For this purpose it was necessary to create new values.[2] As for the definition of this object, even Gökalp himself was not sure at the beginning. He confessed that *Yeni Hayat* was a movement only imperfectly defined, without any clear object or programme. He could get no further than the vague statement that it was necessary to work "with scientific methods and for the sake of the fatherland."[3]

As years went by he became clearer as to the object of his movement, to which he commenced to give the name of Turkism (*Türkçülük*). He realized that the "new life" towards which he was groping was "national life". He explained that this movement was not philosophical or speculative, but that it was founded on positive scientific knowledge, especially on the teachings of modern sociology. It was not possible to create new values,[4] but the object of Turkism was "to seek for the (Turkish) national culture" (*millî harsı aramak*), i.e., to bring to light what was hidden in the soul of the nation.[5] In the course of generations the Turks had

---

[1] G.K., 8; reprinted in Y.M., 25, pp. 482b–485a.

[2] Cf. G. Le Bon: "Ce qui importe dans l'histoire des peuples, ce ne sont ni les révolutions, ni les guerres . . . ce sont les changements dans les idées fondamentales" (*Lois psychologiques de l'évolution des peuples*, Paris, 1898, p. 140-1).

[3] Y.M., 25, pp. 481b–484a.

[4] As he still wrote in 1914 in his essay *Türk Milleti ve Turan* (T., p. 48). K.M., 25, p. 481b; 27, pp. 1a–3b.

drifted away from their national traditions and adopted the cultures of other peoples.

> We succeeded in conquering many places,
> But spiritually we were conquered in all of them.[1]

The Turks occupied vast territories from China to Byzantium, but they did not find their own Promised Land, *Kızıl Elma*, a symbolical expression signifying the national ideal and national culture. Turkish military leaders and thinkers largely contributed to the political and intellectual development of other nations.

> The sword of the Turk and likewise his pen
> Have exalted the Arabs, Chinese and Persians.
> He has created a history and a home for every
>     people,
> He has deluded himself for the benefit of others.[2]

It is now the duty of the Turkish people to "know itself",[3] to summon up its own personality—what Gökalp is fond of designating with his favourite term "ideal". He believes that every people has a distinct soul or spirit which, though imperishable, is likely to absorb alien elements. From this defilement, however, the national spirit is destined to shake itself free in order to create its own special culture. It is the function of the Turkish intellectual to extract this "ideal" from the midst of scattered and confused popular traditions, to re-discover the soul of the people which has been lost through the influences of alien cultures. This is the aim of education of the people, which can be defined as the awakening of ideas existing in the subconscious of the nation. Only in this way will it be possible to create again a living national tradition. The Turks have been converted into a "dogmatic" (*kaideci*) nation, which did not build up its culture along its own natural line of development but received ready-made alien values without assimilating them. It is imperative, therefore, to return to Turkish

[1] K.E., p. 22.
[2] K.E., pp. 23–4.
[3] As the sage says in the poem *Kızıl Elma* (K.E., p. 25). See also the title of the well-known poem *Kendine doğru* (Towards Thyself) (K.E., p. 85).

origins. This can be done in two ways : by research into the history
and culture of the ancient Turks (before their conversion to
Islam), and by examining the popular culture which, unlike the
civilization of the upper classes, has remained faithful to its own
origins and character.[1]

Research into Turkish antiquities is a central feature of Gökalp's
work. Very many of his essays deal with the history of the ancient
Turks, their cultural development, their religion, their laws and
their customs. While this investigation is in part carried out for
its own sake, one often feels that there is behind it an ulterior
purpose, which in some places is openly acknowledged, namely,
to make clear the permanent values on which the new Turkish
culture can be based. In this romantic approach Gökalp goes to
amazing extremes. "Other peoples", he writes in one place,[2]
"are compelled, in order to adopt modern civilization, to depart
from their past. But the Turks have only to turn back to their
ancient past."

In order to glorify the ancient Turks in the eyes of his contemporaries, Gökalp devotes much space to describing their
political and cultural greatness. He dilates enthusiastically on the
condition of the far-flung Turkish kingdoms many centuries
before the rise of Islam and the exploits of great Turkish conquerors like Attila, Jenghiz Khan, Timur and Babur, to whom
he adds, with some hesitation, the Ottoman Sultans. He dwells
similarly on the importance of allegedly Turkish peoples like the
Scythians, the Sumerians and the Hittites who, for him, were the
chief representatives of culture in ancient times. Sometimes
Gökalp admits that the Turkishness of these peoples or even their
ethnic kinship with the Turks lacks proper proof.[3] In various
places, however, he reckons them among the ancient Turks. This
view became "official" in the days of Atatürk, as is evidenced,

[1] T., pp. 15–17, 42, 61–2; K.E., pp. 17–35; University lecture *Halk ve
Güzideler* (quoted in Şapolyo, p. 121).
[2] E., p. 155.
[3] Y.M., 33, p. 136b.

for instance, by the names of the two big Government banks in modern Turkey, *Sümer Bank* (Bank of the Sumerians) and *Eti Bank* (Bank of the Hittites).

With the same object of emphasizing the glorious past of the Turkish people, Gökalp is accustomed to include in the Turkish Pantheon men prominent in the Muslim world like Zamakhsharī, Ibn Sīnā (Avicenna), Jalāl ud-Dīn Rūmī and others, who were Turks by origin (and even this is not certain in every case) but who were brought up in a non-Turkish culture, who wrote their works in Arabic or Persian, and who hardly felt themselves to be Turks. Gökalp here contradicts his own fundamental view that a man's nationality is determined not by his race but by his education, his language and his culture. This tendency to enlarge the circle of national worthies, without much regard to historical truth, is found in almost every incipient national movement of modern times.

The ancient Turks were, according to Gökalp, distinguished by a multitude of excellent qualities: open-handed hospitality, modesty, faithfulness, courage, uprightness, and so forth. Especially praiseworthy was their attitude to the peoples subdued by them. Strong as was their love for their own people, remarks Gökalp with astonishing naïveté, they did not oppress other nations. Their God was a god of peace, and the whole object of their rulers was to establish a régime of peace. Devoid of all imperialistic ambitions, the great Turkish conquerors in ancient times sought to unite the Turkish tribes only. Their religion was free from fanaticism and asceticism, while they attached great importance to the aesthetic side of divine worship. The notions of ideal and personality, the basic concepts in the sociology of Gökalp, were not foreign to the Turks of old and found expression in their code of laws (*yasa*). "An unprejudiced historiography will be compelled in the future to admit that democracy and *feminism* (the movement claiming equal rights for women) were born among the Turks." In ancient Turkish society women were held in high respect; they took part

7

in social life, in political affairs, and even in war. The principle of equality was sacred to the ancient Turks and the representatives of the people had a decisive influence on the conduct of Government. The Turkish tribe and village, in contrast with those of the Arabs, are to this day organized on a democratic basis.[1]

This idealized picture is drawn by Gökalp on the strength of scanty and meagre records—Turkish, Chinese and Arabic—from pre-Islamic and early Islamic periods, and especially of researches carried on among primitive Turkish tribes of our own time (Yakuts and others). In drawing conclusions regarding the permanent qualities of the Turks from the accounts given by the Arab writer Jāḥiz in the ninth century he resembles the German romanticist who proves the superiority of the Teutonic stock from the *Germania* of Tacitus. His ideas of the traditional Turkish virtues are very similar to Herder's claim that Germanism means "faithfulness and simplicity, loyalty and courage".[2] Apart from this belief in the noble descent of his nation, Gökalp makes use of another type of myth common to many nationalist ideologies [3] —the myth of its great mission. Just as Turkish history proves to him the moral superiority of his race, he believes that the historical mission of the Turkish nation is "to realize the highest moral virtues and to prove that the sacrifices and heroic deeds which are generally regarded as impossible are not beyond human strength."[4]

Gökalp overlooks the fact that the ancient Turks were primitive tribes who were devoid both of the defects of an advanced civilization and of its virtues. The attempt to return in the twentieth century to the cultural values of a nomadic people of antiquity is obviously absurd. The scientific study of the pre-Islamic Turks which was continued by Turkish scholars after

---

[1] See the historical essays in Y.M., 23 ; 33 ; 34 ; 35 ; 39 ; the poems *Kızıl Elma, Turan, Altın Destan, Ergenekon* (K.E., pp. 13, 23, 109–19); E., pp. 31–6, 138–40, 150–59, 166 ; K.M., 8 ; 33.          [2] H. Kohn, op. cit., p. 442.

[3] For examples, see Fr. Hertz, op. cit., p. 19 ; R. Michels, *Der Patriotismus* (München, 1929), pp. 1–42.          [4] E., pp. 137, 160.

Gökalp's death, though valuable in itself, has added little to the cultural development of modern Turkey.

More realistic was the attempt of Gökalp to make known the national values which are still living among the masses of the Turkish people to-day. For this purpose he demands the establishment of museums for Turkish folklore, ethnography, and archaeology, of libraries containing all available material on the history of Turkish culture, and of a central institute of statistics supplying the necessary data for sociological enquiries into modern Turkey. He also suggests the establishment of a Turcological society and a national theatre and conservatoire, all of which would play an important rôle in reviving Turkish culture.[1]

Following Herder and his school, Gökalp sees sparks of the Turkish national heritage in the various branches of popular culture—in literature, in the arts (music, architecture, handicrafts, dancing, etc.), and in religious customs and moral standards. This culture has been preserved among the people, while the upper classes adopted the Persian-Arab and later the European culture. Now, however, it is the duty of the Turks to fall back on this heritage, to elevate it, and to base on it a new Turkish culture which shall embrace all classes. Only in this way can the most acute problem in the spiritual life of Turkey be solved: the cleavage between the intellectual class and the masses of the people.

## LANGUAGE

Among all questions relating to culture, it was that of language which particularly engaged the attention of Gökalp, as of all apostles of romantic nationalism. It is by reference to language that he is best able to explain his theories with regard to culture and civilization. As already remarked, he looks on language as the touchstone of nationality and regards independence in the sphere of language as a necessary condition to political independence.[2]

[1] K.M., 3; E., pp. 81–7, 132–3.          [2] T., p. 61; Y.M., 70, p. 53c.

From the time when he began to publish articles in the *Genç Kalemler* of Salonika, Gökalp made it his endeavour to write in a simple language which the people could understand. He denied the right of two languages to exist side by side: Ottoman, the language of the administration and of classical literature, which in its vocabulary and grammar was practically a mixture of three languages (Arabic, Persian and Turkish); and Turkish, the everyday language of the common people and also the language of popular literature, disdained by the intellectuals as a coarse and tasteless jargon. From now on it was absolutely necessary that there should be, even for literary purposes, only one language. This should be based on the spoken language of Constantinople, especially as used by the women, who had more than others preserved its native harmony and sweetness.[1]

By breaking down the barrier between the masses and the intellectuals and opening the gates of literature to the whole of the nation, the "new language" would serve to give expression to the national revival. For this purpose it was necessary to purify it of the numerous foreign elements which it had absorbed. Gökalp, however, does not advocate an excessive linguistic purism (*tasfiyecilik*), like Fuat Raif and the members of the circle connected with the *İkdam* newspaper. He opposes the demand of this school for the elimination of all Arabic and Persian words and their replacement by words formed from Turkish roots. In his view, every word familiar to the people and in common use is a national asset. Arabic words like *kalem* (pen), *ders* (lecture), *kitap* (book), *mektep* (school) have become completely assimilated into spoken Turkish, while many words of Turkish origin have been forgotten since the absorption of the equivalent foreign words. Thus, for instance, no trace has been left of the Turkish words *sayrı* (sick), *gözgü* (mirror), *baskıç* (ladder), which have been replaced by the Persian words *hasta*, *ayna*, *merdiven*. Where the Turkish words

[1] T., pp. 31, 47–8; Y.H., p. 15; Y.M., 25, p. 481b; E., pp. 11, 29, 97–8.

have subsisted side by side with the foreign words they have often acquired a particular shade of meaning. Thus *ak*, *kara* (white, black) are to-day used for the most part in connection with abstract subjects, whereas *beyaz*, *siyah*, meaning the same thing but borrowed from foreign languages, are mainly used to describe material objects. Another sign that words of this kind have become thoroughly acclimatized in Turkish is the change which has taken place in their pronunciation or their meaning. The Persian word *nardubān* (ladder) is pronounced in Turkish *merdiven* and the Arabic *bakara* (pulley) is pronounced *makara*; *pāra* which means "piece" in Persian has in Turkish the sense of "money", and the meaning of the Arabic word *shafaq* is transformed from "dusk" to "dawn". These changes are not just "mistakes" (*galatat*), as they are regarded by the purists, but a proof of the assimilative power of the Turkish language. By rights these words should be written as they are pronounced and not as they are spelt in their language of origin.

There is no sense in rejecting words like these, which have become part and parcel of the vernacular, merely because they have been borrowed from foreign languages. To change these words for old Turkish words or for new words formed from Turkish roots would be equivalent to banishing from the language living elements and introducing into it words more strange and unintelligible to the common people than the Arabic and Persian. Instead of promoting simplicity, clearness and natural expression, the result would be the opposite.[1]

Purging the Turkish language of foreign elements must be carried out on different principles from these. First of all a distinction must be made between scientific and similar terms (*ıstılah*) and other words (*lûgat*). Gökalp proposes to accept such terms only from the Islamic languages, Arabic and Persian, which hitherto had been the source of scientific terminology for the Turkish language. He later adds the condition that such terms

---

[1] Y.H., p. 15; E., pp. 10, 99–107.

should not be compounds but single words, e.g. *hayatiyat* (biology) instead of *ilm-i hayat*, *gariziyat* (physiology) instead of *ilm-i manafi-ülaza*, etc. At the same time he points out that it would be preferable to create such terms, wherever possible, from Turkish roots. He is also willing, especially in his later essays, to accept European words for modern ideas, such as *tiyatro, roman, telefon, şimendifer* (railway), *vapur* (steam-boat). On the other hand he strongly insists on the elimination of all foreign words which have not become rooted in common speech and for which there are, or can easily be formed, synonyms from a Turkish root. An end should be put, in his opinion, to the literary licence which permits the indiscriminate use of synonyms from various languages, such as Turkish *gece*, Persian *şab*, Arabic *layl* (night) or Turkish *su*, Persian *āb*, Arabic *mā'* (water), and so forth.

As the Turkish language will lose a large part of its vocabulary through this process, it will be necessary to replenish it. For this purpose Gökalp proposes to admit into the literary language words from the spoken language and from local dialects in Turkey, though he is not in favour of receiving words from Turkish languages spoken outside the boundaries of Turkey. Only if the required word cannot be found in sources is it permissible to create new words, always of course according to the rules of the Turkish language. Regarding language as a self-developing living organism, Gökalp repeatedly warns against excessive interference by Government institutions in carrying out this process, as this would lead to artificiality and destruction of the beauty of the language.[1]

While in the purging of the Turkish vocabulary Gökalp proceeds with great caution, he denounces without mercy all the grammatical and syntactical formations which Ottoman-Turkish adopted from other languages, especially Arabic and Persian. The foreign plural forms like *zubat* or *zabitan* instead of *zabitler* (officers) must be eliminated. Only those foreign words in the

T., pp. 7, 11–13; Y.H., p. 23; E., pp. 100, 107, 116–19.

plural form are to be admitted which are treated in Turkish as singulars and to which the Turkish plural termination can be added, such as *amele* (workman), *talebe* (pupil), *evlât* (child). The Persian *ızafat* (genitive) construction is also to be abolished; instead of *şuera-i cedide* (new poets) one must say *yeni şairler*. In the same way the Arabic participial forms must be discarded and *muciz* (miraculous), for example, must be replaced by either *icazlı* or *icazcı*. Foreign endings must be replaced by Turkish; *serbestlik* (freedom) must be used instead of *serbesti*, *taçlı* (crowned) instead of *taçdar*, and so forth. The only exceptions are the Persian terminations *-name* and *-hane*, since the words which take them have become absorbed into the common language, and especially the adjective-forming termination *-î*, which cannot yet be dispensed with. Foreign adverbs and conjunctions should also be replaced by Turkish.

Gökalp sums up his requirements in the matter of linguistic reform in the triple formula: modernization and Europeanization of the language in respect of notions, Islamization in respect of scientific terms, and Turkification in respect of all other words, and of grammar, syntax and orthography.[1]

Gökalp himself as a rule writes in a clear and simple style and strives to avoid both Turkish archaisms [2] on the one hand and Persian and Arabic grammatical and syntactical formations on the other. At the same time he freely uses Arabic and Persian words and also forms numerous new terms from roots taken from these languages. He has a special fondness for forming abstract terms by adding *-î* or *-iyet* to an Arabic word, e.g. *seciyevî* (characteristic), *müratebevî* (hierarchical), *şeyiyet* (objectivity), *asriyet* (modernism); by adding Arabic and Persian prefixes, as in *lâ-mukaddes* (profane), *nev-teşekkül* (newly formed); by the use of Arabic verbal nouns as *temdin*, *tahris*, *takdis* (making civilized,

---

[1] T., p. 13; E., pp. 109–14.
[2] Such as the termination *-dek* instead of *kadar* (until) (K.E., pp. 33, 35), which is not very frequent in his writings.

cultured, sacred) and of Arabic endings, e.g. in *ferdiyen-nefsî* (individually subjective). Characteristic is his rendering of the Kantian "categorical imperative" by *makulevî memur bih*. Sometimes he freely interchanges terms borrowed from Arabic-Persian with European or Turkish ones, e.g. *tesanütçülük* or *solidarizm*, *maderzad lisan* or *ana dili* (mother-tongue). In his later writings he shows a marked tendency to replace many terms taken from the Islamic languages by European words. The régime which at first he denominates *imamî* is called in his last book *teokrasi*; instead of *içtimaiyat* which is found in all his earlier writings he uses the word *sosyoloji*, etc.

The development of the Turkish language after Gökalp's death did not follow the lines laid down by him. The elimination of the foreign elements from the grammar and the syntax was, it is true, realized to a large extent. In respect of vocabulary, however, his original suggestion that new terms be taken from Islamic languages was not observed, and the language was flooded with European terms. On the other hand, under the Republic the tendency prevailed to introduce Turkish words to replace even Arabic and Persian words which had become completely acclimatized in Turkish. Thus *mektep* (school) is in official language called to-day *okul*; *vekâlet* (Ministry) has changed to *bakanlık*; *muallim* (teacher) has become *öğretmen*, etc. There has been a strong tendency to revive Turkish words known only to scholars.[1] These changes in the vocabulary have gone so far that a Turkish youth to-day has to use a dictionary to understand fully the works of Gökalp written only thirty years ago.

The introduction in 1928 of the Latin script instead of the Arabic was another innovation in which Atatürk went beyond the limits Gökalp had laid down for language reform. Gökalp, at least in his Constantinople period, explicitly demanded the preservation of the old script, which he regarded as one of the

---

[1] See, for instance, the Constitution of the Republic in its new version as adopted by Act of Parliament in 1945.

major links between the Turks and the other Muslim nations.[1]
No longer vitally concerned with these relations, Atatürk showed
more consistency by introducing a script which was more suitable
for the phonetics of the Turkish language and easier to teach to
the illiterate masses of the people.

## LITERATURE AND ART

The Ottoman literature (the literature of the *Divans*, the
*Tanzimat* and *Servet-i Fünun*) remained strange to the masses
of the Turkish people, who did not understand its language.
Moreover its form and content were not genuinely Turkish but
an imitation of Persian and, from the middle of the nineteenth
century, of French literature.

The prosody most commonly used in Ottoman poetry was the
Arabic-Persian *aruz* (*'arūḍ*), a quantative metrical system. It had
already been pointed out by Ziya Pasha and Cevdet Pasha [2] that
this prosody was not suitable for Turkish owing to the lack of
long vowels in that language. The *aruz* found no place in popular
poetry, the composers of which went on using the ancient Turkish
"syllabic" metres which count the syllables without making any
distinction between long and short (*parmak usulü, parmak hisabı*,
or *hece vezni*). From the days of Nedim in the eighteenth century
a number of writers of *Divans* also composed a few poems in these
metres, but the *aruz* retained its supremacy in Ottoman literature.
Gökalp and his fellow-Turkists strove to eliminate completely the
foreign metres, which in their view also led to an excessive use of
Persian constructions in Ottoman poetry. The modern poet
writing in a syllabic metre should refrain from inventing new
forms which did not suit the taste of the people, such as the
measure of $6 + 6$ syllables in every line (borrowed from the
French Alexandrine). Gökalp himself, while writing his early
poems including the celebrated *Turan* in the *aruz*, used syllabic
metres in his later works. His example was generally followed;

[1] T., p. 33.        [2] According to Gökalp (Y.M., 40, p. 262b).

practically all Turkish poetry nowadays is written in syllabic metres.[1]

The same artificiality which Gökalp found in the metre of the *aruz*, he also criticizes in the content of Ottoman poetry. As its subjects and similes are borrowed from the tradition of other nations it does not, in his opinion, express the feelings of the Turkish people. Whereas, for example, popular literature in dealing with the love motive usually takes for its subject the love-story of a man and a woman and gives it a happy ending in marriage, the poetry of the *Divans*, in imitation of Persian poetry, deals with the tribulations of homosexual love. Turkish humour which found expression so forcibly and naturally in the tales of Nasrettin Hoca and the poems and anecdotes of members of the Bektashi order of dervishes is not reflected in Ottoman literature. The refinements of satirical poets such as Sururi of Kani appear artificial and far-fetched compared with them. It is now the duty of Turkish poets to turn their backs on these foreign influences. They should learn only "technique" from the West, but poetical inspiration and aesthetic taste should come to them from the heritage of the Turkish people. They should search out all the treasures of Turkish popular literature—proverbs, legends and folk-songs, the writings of popular poets like Karacaoğlan, Kaygusuz, Yunus Emre, the hymns of the dervishes, the romances *Aşık Garip*, *Aşık Kerem*, *Şah İsmail*, *Köroğlu* and *Korkut Dede*, the stories of *Nasrettin Hoca*, the *Karagöz* shadow puppet theatre, and the plays of the *Orta Oyunu*.

The same applies to other branches of art. National music, architecture and craftsmanship, Gökalp thinks, cannot be created save by the combination of the traditions still living in the Turkish people with the "technique" of the West. The scope of this term, it would seem, is not clear to Gökalp himself. Metre, for instance, is not included by him in technique, as explained above. On the other hand, the organic connection between the form of every

[1] T., p. 17; E., pp. 29–30, 125–6; Y.M., 8, p. 156; 40, p. 262b–c.

artistic creation and its content is not sufficiently realized by Gökalp.[1]

After Gökalp's death Atatürk strongly and repeatedly urged Turkish artists to adopt Western standards. Mustafa Kemal's intervention in favour of European music is well known. In the modern artistic activities, which considerably increased under the Republic, the general trend has been to follow Western patterns, and the attempts to revive Turkish national traditions have not been conspicuously successful.

### PATRIOTISM AND INTERNATIONALISM

The nationalist ideal is the central feature of Gökalp's political views. A glowing patriotism is revealed by the poems which he wrote in the long period of almost uninterrupted warfare (1912–22)—the Balkan wars,[2] the First World War[3] and Atatürk's Anatolian War.[4]

Gökalp does not agree with the liberal concept of Western Europe that "religion, morality and international law, of course, demand that the policy of a nation should keep within certain bounds and that loyalty to the nation should not transgress them."[5] Far from restraining Turkish nationalism, Islam is in Gökalp's opinion a factor which strengthens patriotic sentiment even in its aggressive forms. For this view he finds support in the Islamic conception of *Jihād*, the Holy War against the unbelievers, and the stress laid by Muḥammad on the fraternity of the faithful (and not on the brotherhood of all men). Ethics too are, in Gökalp's opinion, not supra-national. Since the nation is the source of and the model for all ethical values, morality (*ahlâk*) is for him identical with love of the country and service of the nation.[6]

---

[1] T., pp. 17, 31, 61–2; Y.M., 8, p. 156; 60, pp. 142b–143c; K.M., 3; E. pp. 30–31, 51, 127–31, 134–6.
[2] K.E., pp. 95–8, 125–7, etc.
[3] K.E., pp. 128–32, etc.
[4] Y.H., pp. 55, 57, etc.
[5] Fr. Hertz, op. cit., p. 24.
[6] Y.M., 40, p. 262c and elsewhere.

What is duty? A voice that comes down from
   the throne of God,
Reverberating the consciousness of my nation.
I am a soldier, it is my commander,
I obey without question all its orders.
With closed eyes
I carry out my duty.[1]

In the system of Gökalp, who looks upon nationalism as the
supreme ideal, there is no room for the absolute value of the
individual, which is axiomatic in Western civilization. The
individual who, according to his definition, is the self-centred ego
can never serve as a moral ideal.[2] Personality also, as we have seen,
is worthy of honour and esteem only because it represents and
reflects society, i.e. the nation.

The same superiority which Gökalp assigns to the nation vis-à-
vis the individual is attributed to it also in relation to groups of
greater magnitude than itself. In the scale of ideals he gives to
humanity the last place, after the country, the guild and the
family. The *ümmet*, the international Islamic community, is not
mentioned at all in this essay, which appeared in 1918.[3] Towards
all international watchwords Gökalp adopts an attitude of suspicion and coolness. An international society, he thinks, cannot be
established until all nations have acquired complete independence.
He sneers at the hopes built by certain Turkish circles, after the
end of hostilities in 1918, on the League of Nations which was
then about to be established. Even the Turkish name of this
institution (*Milletler Cemiyeti*) he regards as deceptive, since the
nations have not yet reached any common consciousness which
would enable them to found a real *cemiyet* (society). At the most it
will be possible to establish a *Milletler Camiası*, a weak federation

[1] From the poem *Vazife*, which was first published early in 1915 in I.M.
and later, with some alterations, in Y.H. (p. 12). Fischer (p. 51, *n.* 53) thinks
that Gökalp was influenced by Prussian ideals. Compare also G. Mazzini's view
that "the duties of men to society were prior to their rights, and the idea of duty
implied a supra-natural, religious sanction" (Fr. Hertz, op. cit., p. 385).

[2] Y.M., 43, p. 322b.

[3] Cf. Durkheim's "hierarchy" of ideals in *Educ. morale*, pp. 84 *sq.*

of nations belonging to the same civilization, but devoid of the forces which form the basis of any ideal, namely prestige (*icaz*) and sanction (*teyit*).[1] So long as this international body has no legislative, executive and judicial powers and no army and fleet stronger than the forces of its member-States, the individual State should not be led astray by these international and cosmopolitan slogans, but should rely on its own national strength.[2]

Gökalp is particularly suspicious of these Western catchwords, because the Turks have learnt by experience since the Middle Ages that when Europeans speak of an international federation they mean a compact between Christian nations, and that the object of every international statute of this kind is to confer rights and privileges on these countries only. However, this situation may change since the acceptance of non-Christian nations into the orbit of European civilization shows that this civilization is in a process of transition from religious to secular international-ism, founded on positive science and open to members of all creeds.[3]

The wars of the European Powers against Turkey from the subjugation of Tripoli (1911) to the entry of the Allies into Con-stantinople and of the Greeks into Smyrna and Central Anatolia (1919–21) aroused in the Turks a bitter hatred against the West which, as we have seen, found expression in the writings of Gökalp, especially in his poems.[4] It is to be noted, however, that as he recedes farther from his Islamic standpoint he is more and more inclined to lay the blame for this European aggressiveness not on Christian religious fanaticism but on the political imperial-ism of the Western powers. Gökalp is convinced that the day of empires is past and that sooner or later all the nations subject to this kind of régime will rise in a struggle for national freedom.

[1] For the particular sense of these terms in Gökalp's writings, see p. 52.
[2] E., p. 90; K.M., 11.
[3] T., pp. 8–10; Y.M., 35, pp. 163c–164a; E., pp. 78–9.
[4] Y.M., 37, p. 202b; K. E., pp.81–2, 90–92, 121, 128–132; K.M., 5; 33; E., p. 76.

The Turks, who have long since abandoned a policy of imperial-
ism,[1] are opposed to the transfer of Muslim lands to a mandatory
rule which is only another name for a colonial régime. Until
empires have vanished from the world, Gökalp argues—evidently
under the prompting of the anti-imperialist declarations of the
Russian revolution—peace will not be established in the world.
It is imperative that the right of every nation to establish its own
independent State should be recognized.[2]

### TURANISM

While empires made up of various nations are disintegrating,
there is on the other hand a striving for union between countries
with populations belonging to the same nationality (Italy, Germany, etc.). This tendency will, in the opinion of Gökalp, lead in
the course of time to the union of all the Turks in their vast
territories which stretch from the Balkans to the Chinese border
and which form what Gökalp and his friends were used to call
*Turan.*

In Constantinople the Turanian movement started after the
revolution of 1908–9 at the instigation of young Turks from
Russia. Gökalp finds the first manifestation of this movement in
the poem *Turan* by Hüseyinzade Ali who, as already mentioned,
was influenced by Pan-Slavism. A greater impression was made
on the Turkish intellectuals by the poem of the same title published by Gökalp in 1911 in the Salonika newspaper *Rumeli* over
the signature of Demirdaş, and also in the magazine *Genç Kalemler*
over the signature of Tevfik Sedat. The last couplet of this poem
was taken as the motto of Turanism:

> The country of the Turks is not Turkey, nor yet Turkestan,
> Their country is a broad and everlasting land—Turan.[3]

---

[1] See the poem *Ötügen Ülkesi* (K.E., pp. 86–7), in which an ancient Turkish
ruler expresses Gökalp's ideas in opposition to new conquests and in favour
of the economic development of the country.

[2] Y.M., 35, pp. 162b–164a; E., pp. 38, 67, 78, 89–90.

[3] K.E., p. 13.

In the succeeding years Gökalp,[1] Halide Edib and their associates dreamt of a union of all the Turks under a single ruler who would renew the days of Attila, Jenghiz Khan and Timur.

Gökalp lays it down as indisputable that all the Turkish peoples (*ulus*), the Ottomans, the Turks of Azerbaijan and the Crimea, the Turcomans, the Kirghiz, the Uzbeks, the Kipchaks, etc., potentially form one nation. It is true that in respect of racial type there are great differences between them, but, as stated above, in Gökalp's opinion race does not determine nationality. The important thing is that all Turks have a common culture. All of them, with the exception of the distant Yakuts, are Muslims, they have similar customs and institutions, and their language is fundamentally the same. Though Turkish is divided into many dialects, most Turks, according to Gökalp, can understand one another.[2]

Since the beginning of this century, however, the Turks of Russia have shown leanings to a cultural separatism. Under the influence of socialistic ideas certain Turkish circles in Russia endeavoured to develop their own regional literature and to transform their local dialect into a literary language. The Russian authorities, whose policy was to weaken the bond between the Turks of their country and the Ottomans, encouraged them to pursue this course. On the other hand the centripetal tendency showed itself strongest in the Crimea and the Caucasus, where Ottoman was becoming the literary language. Papers like *Tercüman* in the Crimea, *Şelâle* in Baku and even certain papers in Bokhara and Ferghana were written in a language close to Ottoman Turkish. The books and papers which before the First World War were sent in large quantities from Constantinople to the Turkish centres in Russia helped to knit closer these cultural ties. An important link was also constituted by the numerous young Turks who came from Russia to study in Constantinople and

[1] See his poems *Kızıl Elma* and *Yeni Attilâ* (K.E., pp. 17–35, 90–92).
[2] T., pp. 43–5; Y.H., p. 10; Y.M., 51, p. 482b–c; 62, pp. 184c–185a.

afterwards returned to their own land as bearers of Ottoman culture.[1]

With the outbreak of the First World War, in which Russia fought against the Ottoman Empire, the Turanists hoped that the hour had arrived for the liberation of the "northern" Turks from the Tsarist yoke and for their union with the Ottoman Empire. Gökalp opened his poem *Kızıl Destan* which he wrote in the first months of the war with the couplet:

> The land of the enemy shall be devastated,
> Turkey shall be enlarged and become Turan.[2]

These hopes were dashed to the ground by the defeat of the Ottoman armies, but they revived again after the exit of Russia from the war and the revolution of the Bolsheviks, who abandoned all imperialistic policies and promised freedom to the subject peoples. In an article published in April 1918, Gökalp encouraged the Turks in Russia to seize their unique opportunity for obtaining full independence. He advised them to create gradually a large state with a central government and with Ottoman-Turkish for its official language. For this purpose they would have to appoint a leader, a supreme commander for all their armies who would fix his capital in the Caucasus, in Turkestan, or in Kazakstan. This heaven-sent leader, who might originate among either the Turks of Russia or the natives of Turkey, would undertake the sacred task of liberating Turan.[3]

A leader of this kind, such as the Ottoman Turks found in the following year in the person of Mustafa Kemal, was not vouchsafed to the Turks of Russia. Enver Pasha, one of the leaders of the Union and Progress Party, attempted to raise a revolt against the Soviet Government in Turkestan, but was killed in battle in August 1922. The Bolshevik armies suppressed every separatist movement among the Turks in Russia, and the Turanian goal again appeared as distant as in the days before 1914.

[1] Y.M., 31, 83a–c; 40, pp. 262c–263b; T., pp. 45–7.
[2] K.E., p. 128.    [3] Y.M., 38, pp. 233a–235a.

Even before this, however, Gökalp had ceased to support the extreme demand of this movement for the political union of all Turks. At the beginning of 1918 he declared that the first task was to unite all the Turkish peoples on the cultural side alone. The chief means for bringing about this unity was the adoption of the language of Constantinople—the most highly developed, the richest and the most euphonious among the Turkish dialects—as the national language, just as some Pan-Slavists believed that Russian should become the universal language of the Slavs. Should a number of separate Turkish States arise after the conclusion of the war, this cultural unity would serve as a foundation on which could be built, in the course of years, a political unity, as had been done in Italy and Germany. In this development Ottoman Turkey would perform the same function as had been performed by Prussia in the German unification movement.[1]

In his last writings Gökalp further narrowed down the Turanian programme. Even cultural unity could be realized under present conditions only among the *Oğuz* Turks, i.e. those in Turkey, Azerbaijan, Iran and Khwarizm, who all had a common literary heritage (the poet Fuzuli, the *Korkut Dede* tales, popular stories like *Şah İsmail*, *Aşık Garip*, *Aşık Kerem*, *Köroğlu*, etc.). There could be no thought of realizing in our days the Turanian aim, which was only an inspiring ideal, a vision of the distant future.[2]

This was also the view of Atatürk, who carefully abstained from any action which might irritate his ally Soviet Russia, and who tried to concentrate the whole energies of his nation on the development of the country within its new boundaries. It is significant that in 1927 the *Türk Ocağı*, one of the objects of which was to establish connections with the Turks outside Turkey, altered its programme. Paragraph (2) of its constitution now read: "The field of operations of the *Türk Ocağı* extends only to the boundaries of the Turkish Republic."[3]

---

[1] Y.M., 31, pp. 82a–84a; 51, p. 482a–c.  [2] E., pp. 22–5.
[3] *Oriente Mod.*, XXIII (1943), p. 387.

8

In spite of this official disavowal, the Turanian movement did not disappear entirely. During the Second World War, and especially after the German invasion of Russia, renewed activity was shown in Turkey by a secret revolutionary society which aimed at the political union of all Turks. At the end of 1944, however, this racialist movement was suppressed by the Ankara Government and its leaders brought to trial before a military court.[1]

## MINORITIES

The Young Turk revolution of 1908 promised equality to all Ottoman subjects without distinction of religion and race. These promises, however, were never carried out. Differences of interest and of political outlook were too deep to be smoothed over, and the traditional enmity between the Turks and the other communities, particularly the non-Muslims (Greeks, Armenians and Jews) still persisted. The Muslims' feeling of superiority over and contempt for these communities was mixed with a certain jealousy of their achievements, and this attitude towards the *gâvur* (unbeliever) appears also in Gökalp's early views on this question.[2] The non-Muslim communities, he writes, which had no part in the political life of the Empire and were exempt from military service, have always been able to concentrate their attention on their economic interests and, thanks to the large measure of autonomy granted to them by the Turks, on the development of their social life. In recent times they have shown greater readiness and ability than their Muslim neighbours to adapt themselves to European civilization. Gökalp consoles himself and his co-religionists with the reflection that the Muslims will eventually surpass the other communities in economic progress, as they will

[1] See Alexander Henderson, *The Pan-Turanian Myth in Turkey Today* (in *The Asiatic Review* (January 1945), pp. 88–92).
[2] See *Genç Kalemler*, July–August 1911.

carry out modernization more thoroughly and on a larger scale.[1]

As mentioned above, Gökalp does not agree with the liberal circles which advocate the establishment of an "inter-communal" State, all citizens of which would regard themselves as Ottomans. He is convinced that the only sound course is to establish a multi-national State in which all the different communities are recognized as separate nationalities. He hopes that after the Muslim Turks have reached the stage of national consciousness they will respect the claims of the other nationalities in the Ottoman Empire. On the other hand, the latter must understand that they are face to face with a strong and united Turkish nation and that it will be in their interest to cease from invoking the aid of foreign powers and to come to an agreement with the Turks.[2]

Gökalp soon lost faith in the possibility of such a multi-national State and came to the conclusion that only a State consisting of one nation can exist.[3] One can notice this development in Gökalp's views in his changing attitude towards the most important non-Turkish element in the Ottoman Empire—the Arabs. Shortly before the outbreak of the First World War he suggested the establishment of a bi-national State (to be called the Turco-Arab State) under the Ottoman Caliph.[4] The revolt of the Sharīf Husain and the defeat of the Turks on the Palestine front prompted him to offer greater concessions to the Arabs. In 1918 he proposed a federation or confederation of two independent States, Turkish Anatolia and "Arabistan". This union, he said, was natural for geographical as well as religious reasons and vital for the defence of both nations. It would be beneficial especially for the Arabs who, lacking civil and military organization, would be conquered by European powers as soon as they separated themselves from their Turkish brothers.[5] The defeat of the Ottoman Empire in

---

[1] G.K., 8.

[2] T., pp. 31–2.

[3] T., p. 58. See also pp. 72–4 above.

[4] T., pp. 52–3.

[5] Y.M., 35, p. 163b–c.

1918 relieved Gökalp of the need of worrying about the fate of the Arabs. Except for a tiny Arab minority which remained within the borders of the Turkish State, all Arab provinces were lost.

Regarding the other minorities Gökalp distinguishes between Muslims and non-Muslims. His principle was that the Turkish nation was composed only of Turkish-speaking Muslims. That meant that the Greeks, Armenians and Jews who lived in Turkey were Turks only in respect of citizenship but not of nationality. Gökalp's opinion presumably was that they would remain a foreign body in the national Turkish State. Although he was in favour of granting the minorities a certain cultural autonomy, he apparently objected to the continuation of the Ottoman *millet* system, which gave all non-Muslim communities large-scale autonomy in their legal, social and educational affairs. An indication of this can be found in his demand for the abolition of the Pious Foundations, both Christian and Muslim.

Gökalp's attitude with regard to the large Kurdish minority is not clear. As would be natural for a man who grew up in a largely Kurdish province, he hopes that the two Muslim nations, the Turks and the Kurds, will live in peace and harmony. Since, however, he does not explicitly suggest giving the Kurds cultural autonomy, he seems to anticipate that they would be assimilated by the Turks.[1]

The policy of the Turkish Republic tried to achieve Gökalp's ideal of a homogeneous Turkish nation. The majority of the Greek population was exchanged against Turks, and the bulk of the Armenians left Turkey gradually. The remaining non-Muslim minorities, now greatly reduced in numbers and no longer causing a serious problem, were integrated into the social fabric of the Republic. The Kurdish revolts in Eastern Anatolia were suppressed and a determined policy of assimilation of the Kurds was adopted.

[1] Y.M., 35, p. 163b–c; 51, pp. 481a, 482b; K.M., 1; 33.

### FORM OF GOVERNMENT

The political régime which Gökalp desires to see established in Turkey is a national democracy. He regards democracy and nationalism, the dominant watchwords of the First World War, as two ideals closely linked with one another. Both are based on the same principle of equality—the former on equality within the national society, the latter on equality among nations. Only in a homogeneous nation, and not in a heterogeneous society like the Ottoman Empire, is it possible to establish a true democracy in which the rulers represent and serve the nation.[1]

Gökalp's idea of democracy is rather different from liberal conceptions. It is true that he calls the régime which he advocates *halkçılık*, which he means to be a translation of the term "democracy". In fact, however, he desires to place supreme control in the hands not of the masses of the people (*halk*) but of the nation (*millet*), and more precisely of the national élite (*güzideler*), who have to govern in the interests of the people. He states categorically that in his opinion democracy is not the rule of the ignorant masses (*avam*) but of the élite "who are the people because they say 'we are the people.'"[2] In the democratic society, as Gökalp sees it, everybody, without distinction of class or occupation, enjoys the same political status, on condition that he accepts the principle of legal equality of all members of the nation. The only way to establish the democratic régime is not by putting an end to the rule of the upper classes, but by applying the principle that "democracy means turning the whole people into aristocrats".[3]

Gökalp regards the feudalism which came into being during the last centuries of the Ottoman Empire as an important stage in the

---

[1] Y.M., 32, p. 102a; 33, p. 123b–c; 35, p. 162a.

[2] See his University lecture *Halk ve Güzideler* (1918) (quoted in Şapolyo, p. 123). Cf. F. Meinecke, *Weltbürgertum und Nationalstaat* (München, 1915), p. 24: "Die geistig oder politisch führende Schicht einer Nation hat . . . immer die Neigung, sich selbst mit der Nation zu identifizieren."

[3] Y.M., 32, p. 104a; E., p. 62.

development from the absolute rule of the Sultans to the constitutional régime of the Young Turks. The feudal lords (*derebeyleri*) of that period succeeded, unlike the holders of *ziyamet* (military fiefs) in the preceding period, in obtaining official recognition of their authority and in transmitting it to their descendants. Thus, for the first time in Ottoman history, an aristocracy with considerable influence on the affairs of the State came into existence. It indicated, in Gökalp's opinion, a fundamental change in the structure of the Ottoman Empire, in which even the holders of the highest positions of State had been regarded as Slaves of the Sultan (*kapıkulu*).[1]

Gökalp was led to adopt his views on democracy by certain social developments in Turkey. The democratic régime of the West was the fruit of long struggles between the Third Estate and the feudal rulers, whereas in Turkey no (Muslim) bourgeoisie had yet been formed and the masses had not yet developed a political consciousness. Abdul Hamid's autocratic régime was overthrown by a group of Army officers and of intellectuals, the majority of whom belonged to the class of civil servants and did not represent any of the major economic groups of the nation. Furthermore, they were not placed in power by any democratic election. The right of this "élite" to speak in the name of the people was based only on their own inner conviction that they understood the needs of the people and would work in its interests.

This fact explains the central position which Gökalp allots in his democratic State to the Leader, whom he regards as a kind of head of the "élite." Already in 1918, as mentioned above, he was dreaming of a great military leader (*reis*) who would liberate the Turks in Russia and establish a large Turanian Empire. The clergy would recognize him as sent by God and the intelligentsia as a genius and national hero. In this period of serious danger for the existence of the nation, it would be imperative to give the Leader absolute powers. Only after victory had been won and the

[1] Y.M., 32, pp. 103a–104b.

people had been trained for self-government could the Leader hand over his power to the people.[1]

These words were written about a year before Mustafa Kemal reached Samsun and began preparations for the War of Independence (May 1919). Gökalp, according to one of his friends,[2] greeted with enthusiasm the first news of Kemal Pasha's movement, which he received during his exile in Malta, and urged every patriotic Turk to join it. After returning to Turkey he praised the Ghazi as Father of the People, Saviour (*münci*) of the Nation, and the personification of the national ideal.[3] But for the splendid victories of the Ghazi, Gökalp writes in those days, Turkism would have remained a dead letter. The League for the Defence of the Rights of Anatolia and Rumeli, Mustafa Kemal's party, was carrying out the political programme of Turkism unconsciously. Therefore it was the duty of every Turkist to support this party. (Several leaders of the Turkist movement, such as Mehmet Emin and Akçoraoğlu, had already in April 1921 gone to Ankara and joined Mustafa Kemal.) On the eve of the elections to the Great National Assembly in 1923, Gökalp wrote a pamphlet called *Doğru Yol* (The Right Way), in which he explained the programme of this party and showed that the principles of the Ghazi's policy conformed to the programme of Turkism.[4]

In accordance with his theories on élite and geniuses Gökalp tries to prove that a national leader like the Ghazi can create a "collective consciousness" and so carry out with one word or by one speech far-reaching reforms. "Everything is possible; only demand, give the order", he calls to the Ghazi.[5] This view, it

[1] Y.M., 38, pp. 234c–235a.

[2] Ağaoğlu Ahmet in his article *Ziya Gökalp Bey*, published in *Türk Yurdu* and quoted in Şapolyo (p. 140).

[3] K.M., 21; 26. Gökalp had written similar eulogies earlier on Young Turk leaders, such as Talât Pasha and Enver Pasha (Y.H., pp. 39–40). A few years after he had addressed Talât Pasha with the words "Without thee the nation will become an orphan" (Y.H., p. 39), he asks the new leader, Mustafa Kemal, "Don't forsake (the nation) like a wretched orphan" (K.M., 21).

[4] E., pp. 13–14, 170–71.

[5] E., p. 65; K.M., 20.

should be pointed out, is in complete contrast with the evolutionary theories which he had held previously and which he had summarized only a few years earlier in a poem in honour of Mustafa Necip:

> You know that radical change is not the work of a moment,
> All its hopes depend on time.[1]

It was the political events of those years which led Gökalp to this change of outlook. Up to the period of Mustafa Kemal, Gökalp remained faithful to the views which he had imbibed during his confinement in the Constantinople prison, namely, that no stable constitutional Government could be established in Turkey before the people had been educated for democracy.[2] Events, however, did not allow this process to be completed. "Before the nation had time to learn and to think, it was compelled to rise and save its honour and rights." [3] The Ghazi who led the nation in its War of Independence must now "teach the people, direct it in its work and gradually accustom it to democracy".[4] It is interesting to note that Muḥammad 'Abduh, the great Egyptian reformer, also in the beginning advocated Parliamentary democracy but in later years reached the conclusion that the necessary reforms could be carried out only by an authoritarian régime under a strong ruler.[5]

Gökalp's language betrays a distinct undercurrent of apprehension lest the new régime should have been founded before the people were prepared for it. It is impossible to say definitely whether Gökalp already foresaw that the Ghazi's leadership would turn into an authoritarian rule—albeit a régime working for the good of the nation in accordance with Gökalp's own ideas—and

---

[1] Y.H., p. 42.

[2] These views coincide with those of Gökalp's teacher Durkheim who was "the avowed enemy of all violent upheaval which involved a sudden and serious breach with the past" (M. M. Mitchell in *Political Science Quarterly*, XLVI, p. 95).

[3] K.M., 19.

[4] K.M., 21.

[5] See Osman Amin, *Muhammad 'Abduh* (Cairo, 1944), p. 114–17.

what his attitude would have been if he had lived to see it. In some places Gökalp expresses his opposition to the concentration of legislative and executive functions in the hands of one man and praises the Parliamentary régime, as established in Turkey with the election of the Great National Assembly (*Büyük Millet Meclisi*).[1] He does not, however, go deeply into the question, and it would seem that he does not attach very great importance to the form of Government as long as its policy conformed to the programme of Turkism.

For this reason, and in accordance with his general tendency to adjust his theories to the existing political conditions, Gökalp did not raise the question of the Sultanate till a few months before its abrogation. Enver Behnan Şapolyo and Ali Nüzhet quote some fragments of poems, not known from other sources, which Gökalp wrote during his revolutionary period before 1908, and in which he preaches a rebellion against the tyranny of Abdul Hamid.

> Why we leave to a Sultan every right, I do not know. . . .
> Is the nation not able to govern itself?[2]

> We are the workers in the fields and mills,
> We are this State, this nation, this country.
> Abdicate, Sultan! We are the rulers.[3]

After the Young Turk revolution and the restoration of the constitution Gökalp's attacks on the Sultanate were discontinued. In the patriotic and religious poems which he wrote during the years of war with the Christian Powers he prayed for the Sultan-Caliph, the symbol of the Ottoman State and the spiritual head of the Islamic world.[4] Later, when his political views crystallized in favour of a modern secular State, he came to the conclusion that the Court was one of the major obstacles in the way of the necessary reforms. Until the downfall of the Young Turk régime in 1918, however, he did not dare to display any republican

---

[1] K.M., 25; E., p. 73.
[2] Şapolyo, p. 38.
[3] Ali Nüzhet, p. 20.
[4] K.E., pp. 83, 92.

tendencies. But one of his friends [1] reports that already during the First World War he wanted to turn the Sultan into a kind of President of the Republic. In his writings of this period he strongly opposed every reactionary movement which tried to strengthen the Sultanate at the expense of Parliament and the rights of the people.[2] On his return from Malta he found that the prestige of the Sultan had greatly declined and that the Ghazi, the victorious war leader, had become the most popular figure in Anatolia. Already in the second issue of his weekly *Küçük Mecmua* (June 1922) he published an allegorical poem extolling the sovereignty of the people.

> God's representative (on earth) is the people. . . .  .
> Authority belongs to the people and not to the Sultan. . . .
> To it belongs all power—legislative, judicial and executive.[3]

After the final victory of the Ghazi and the armistice of Mudanya (October 1922) the future of the Sultan's Constantinople Government, which put forward a demand to take part in the forthcoming Peace Conference, was hotly debated in Turkey. In those days Gökalp reminded the people of the sins of the Sultan who for many years had co-operated with Turkey's enemies, the Allied Powers.

> Our leader should not be a secret enemy,
> Our foes' friend must not remain our ruler,
> Save us from this gilded snake.[4]

On 1 November 1922, the Turkish Parliament decided to abolish the Sultanate. Gökalp welcomed this act as an important step towards the transformation of Turkey into a progressive and free State.[5]

While Gökalp supported the change of régime, there is little doubt that he would not have approved of the large degree of

---

[1] Muhittin Birgen, former editor-in-chief of *Tanin* (quoted in the preface to *Altın Işık*).
[2] Y.M., 36, p. 181a–c.
[3] K.M., 2.
[4] K.M., 20 (published 23 October 1922).
[5] K.M., 23 (published 20 November 1922).

State control which was introduced in Turkey after his death. Although he always insisted that the requirements of the nation must take precedence over those of the individual, he was strongly opposed, at least up to the defeat of the Young Turks, to placing excessive power in the hands of the State and to its domination of social, and particularly cultural, life. In his opinion the true rulers are the élite, the "brains of the nation", and the Government should be only the mechanism for carrying out their decisions. Demanding the separation of politics and culture, he wants the State not to intervene in matters of science, art and academic teaching. The only rôle the State should play in this field is to foster free cultural activities by its material assistance. He is also opposed to any State control of the press and to intervention in the activities of the guilds, which, as will be shown later, he regards as initial bodies in the ideal State. His fundamental aim is to educate the people for self-government and progress and to strengthen their initiative and public spirit in place of the indifference and fatalism which had taken root in the Turkish people under the autocracy of the Sultans.[1]

Gökalp's opposition to a totalitarian State was the fruit of his bitter memories of absolute rule in the past as well as of the democratic ideals he had accepted from the West.[2] Mustafa Kemal and his friends, however, considered his suggestions as totally impracticable. They remained loyal to his ideal but adopted other methods of realizing it. Rightly or wrongly they regarded themselves as under the necessity of strengthening the State at the expense of the freedom which the Turkish people had not yet learned to appreciate. In their opinion "the average Turk had to be compelled to be reasonable and progressive and free".[3] In their great enterprise of turning a backward Oriental society rapidly into a strong

---

[1] Y.M., 57, pp. 82c–83c; Y.H., pp. 17, 31; K.M., 19; 33; E., pp. 45, 162; Şapolyo, pp. 119–23.

[2] Durkheim too favoured limiting the functions of the State and did not recognize the State as the main source of moral values.

[3] B. Ward, *Turkey* (Oxford University Press, 1942), p. 57.

and progressive European nation, they did not rely on the initiative
and abilities of the individual, but made the State the controlling
and directing force in all spheres of life, including cultural
activities. A typical example of this policy is the reform of the
Turkish language, a matter very dear to Gökalp. In spite of his
assertions that a language cannot be reformed by acts of Parliament but only by the work of free scholars and writers,[1] the "language revolution" in Atatürk's time and afterwards was carried
through by laws and under Government guidance.[2] Nevertheless,
there can be little doubt that Gökalp's conception of society, the
élite and the Leader prepared the ground for Atatürk's authoritarian régime.

### SOCIALISM AND SOLIDARISM

More than the champions of nationalism in many countries,
particularly in the nineteenth century, Gökalp appreciates the
importance of social problems and tries to find a solution to them
which shall accord with nationalist aims and conceptions.

In his opinion, the Turkish nation cannot progress without
raising the cultural and economic level of the masses, especially
the village population. Following the Russian example he calls
upon the intellectuals "to go to the people", to bring Western
civilization into the Anatolian villages, to establish there schools
and, in his early writings, mosques. The Turkish village must be
saved from the hands of the usurer, the tax-farmer and the grasp-
ing trader. The tithe (*âşar*) should be abolished and an Agricultural Bank and co-operative societies should be founded. In
addition, the Government should enact laws to protect the
workers, and particularly women and children.[3] Gökalp does

[1] Y.M., 57, p. 83c.

[2] Such as the adoption of the Latin alphabet, the publications of the official
Language Committee (*Dil Kurumu*), the creation of the strange *Güneş-Dil
Teorisi* (Sun Theory of Language) and the translation of the Constitution of
the Republic into purer Turkish.

[3] Y.H., p. 14; E., pp. 41, 45; K.M., 20; see also his articles in *İktisadiyat
Mecmuası*, 1916–18.

not close his eyes to the grievances of the masses against the upper classes. In his interesting poem *Esnaf Destam* [1] he praises the workers and artisans who are the "core of the nation", hard-working, honest, patriotic and eager for progress. They have many bitter complaints against the clerical and intellectual leaders who neglect the working classes, and against the rich and the aristocrats who shirk their national duties in the hour of crisis.

> War broke out. We shall sacrifice ourselves for the nation,
> We said. Our blood was spilt freely, but
> Our notables and dignitaries [2] did not join the battle. . . .
> The donation of the rich has to be taken by force, . . .
> Has the country claims only on us? [3]

Nevertheless, Gökalp is strongly opposed to any class struggle and to socialism in all its aspects. His arguments against historical materialism have been mentioned above.[4] His main opposition to Marxism springs fundamentally from his belief that this ideology undermines national unity since it regards only one class, the proletariat, as the true "people" (*halk*). Through this notion socialism leads to discrimination against other classes and attempts to suppress them, the natural outcome of which, in Gökalp's opinion, is civil war and the establishment of an oppressive régime like that of Soviet Russia. A true democracy, as required in the interest of the common people, will not be based on the privileged position of one class but on the equality of all sections of the nation.[5]

Gökalp rightly points out that in the Ottoman Empire a kind of class struggle went on between the "Ottoman" bureaucracy and the "Turkish" masses ruled by them.[6] It does not, of course,

---

[1] K.E., pp. 120–24.

[2] In an article published in Y.M. (32, p. 104a–b) Gökalp uses these words (*eşraf, âyan*) in the meaning of bourgeoisie and aristocracy.

[3] K.E., p. 123. Fichte, whom Gökalp resembles in so many respects, also regards the egoism of the upper classes as one of the main causes of national decline (see Fr. Hertz, op. cit., p. 341).

[4] P. 51.

[5] Y.M., 38, p. 234a; K.M., 25; E., pp. 62, 161.

[6] E., pp. 33–4.

occur to him that a similar clash could happen between the masses and a nationalist bureaucracy.

Despite his antipathy to the Soviet State, Gökalp does not entirely repudiate socialism, but he considers that social conditions in his country are not suitable for such a movement. An industrial proletariat, such as formed the backbone of the socialist movement in Europe, does not yet exist in Turkey. As for the remnants of feudalism and theocracy, Gökalp hopes that the new democratic régime will soon eliminate them entirely. Moreover, Turkey's international position requires a united front of all sections of the nation against its external enemies. Only when the social structure of the Turkish people has changed as a result of industrialization, might there be a chance for socialism. But even then it will have to remain part and parcel of and subject to the general national movement.[1]

The mere abolition of legally and politically privileged classes does not automatically bring about national unity and true democracy as long as acute economic differences continue to exist in the State. For eliminating such differences Gökalp does not, like the socialists, advocate the abolition of private ownership of the means of production and the transference of supreme power to the working class. He tries to find a compromise between capitalism and socialism by means of a plan combining the freedom of the individual and his economic rights with equality and social justice. In this way he hopes to promote peace and co-operation between the different classes. He calls his programme solidarism (*tesanütçülük*) or social democracy (*içtimaî halkçılık*).[2]

This ideology is based on the recognition of both private and public rights of ownership. Private ownership, particularly of the means of production, is to be permitted only on condition that it is used for the good of the community. If, for instance, a factory

---

[1] T., pp. 5, 6, 45, 59; K.M., 25.

[2] On solidarism as a philosophy, see *Le solidarisme* (Paris, 1907) by C. Bouglé, a leading member of Durkheim's school.

is not worked or a field is not cultivated during a certain period, it will become *mahlûl* and fall to the State. Private property is to be regarded as a kind of deposit which society has entrusted to the owners and of which it resumes possession if they do not make the right use of it. In addition, the State will be entitled, if need arises, to expropriate any land or undertaking on payment of compensation to their owners. In this way means of production can be transferred to more suitable managers or can be nationalized without, Gökalp seems to believe, any fear of internal warfare, as happened in Russia. Gökalp apparently takes for granted that the private owners would freely agree or could easily be forced to submit to the will of the Government.

The second principle of solidarism is that unearned increment created by the efforts of society should belong to it and not to private individuals. The huge revenues which would thus accumulate in the public treasury should be spent for two main purposes: (*a*) to carry out comprehensive social reforms, such as general insurance, mutual assistance schemes, free education, etc.; and (*b*) to develop State estates and industries. The profits of these undertakings too will be spent on social reforms and on large-scale public works, such as the electrification of the whole country, public parks, libraries, museums, theatres, etc. When the accumulated capital reaches a sufficient amount Gökalp—with amazing optimism—hopes that the State will be able to abolish taxation or at least to reduce it considerably.[1]

For tracing the development of Gökalp's theory it is interesting to note that in his article published in 1918 he suggests that the capital should be spent for the first purpose, social reforms, only. The programme of State enterprise involved in his second suggestion is mentioned in his book published in 1923, and may have been a result of the Soviet example.

As usual, Gökalp tries to prove that the roots of solidarism can be found in Turkish tradition. In the Ottoman land laws (*arazi*

[1] Y.M., 26, p. 502b; 38, p. 234b; E., pp. 167–8.

*kanunnamesi*), for instance, there are found side by side the two concepts of *tasarruf*, private property, and *rakebe*, corresponding in his opinion to public ownership.[1] Actually it would seem that Gökalp got these ideas from a friend and collaborator who was deeply influenced by the social reform policy (*Sozialpolitik*) and the social democratic movement in Germany. This was Tekin Alp (his original name was M. Cohen) who published in the *Yeni Mecmua* a number of articles on economics, among them several dealing with solidarism.[2] He demanded that the Turkish national movement should not tie itself to the capitalist system which had commenced to develop in the country during the First World War, but should serve the people by means of social, though not socialist or communist, reforms.

Solidarism aims at putting an end to class struggle and at giving everybody equal opportunities for education and work. To attain this end Gökalp demands the abolition of the classes (*sınıf*) into which modern nations are divided, and the substitution for them of occupational unions or guilds (*meslek*) which would promote mutual co-operation throughout the people. Gökalp regards the classes as forming "consumption groups" and considers the deep differences in the consumption levels of the various classes to be contrary to social justice. The guilds, on the other hand, are composed of people in the same occupation. They are the result of the division of labour and the specialization which in Durkheim's opinion are signs of social progress, and they form, therefore, a sound and vital element in the social organism. In this case also Gökalp finds support for his views in the Turkish traditions relating to the *ahi* associations in Seljuq times and the *esnaf loncaları* in the Ottoman Empire. While these associations were mainly composed of artisans, now everybody should be enrolled in a guild. Furthermore, unlike these local associations of the

[1] Y.M., 38, p. 234a.
[2] Y.M., 26, *sq.* Cohen was in 1916–18 assistant and interpreter to the German Professor of Public Finance at the Constantinople University (see Fındıkoğlu, *Türkiyede İktisat Tedrisatı Tarihçesi* (Istanbul, 1946), p. 54).

past the guilds in these days of national planning must cover the whole country. The central bodies of all these organizations are to elect representatives who will form the Central Board of all the guilds. In addition, Labour Offices (*İş Bürolari*) composed of representatives of the various guilds in every town will be established to regulate local economic activities. The guilds will have a wide sphere of activity; they will promote the improvement of working conditions, invite foreign experts to Turkey and send Turkish students abroad, establish co-operatives and stores, and institutions for mutual assistance, health and education. Gökalp attaches particular importance to the maintenance of professional morale. He is said to have published in 1917 a leaflet called *Meslekî Ahlâk Beyannamesi* (Declaration of Professional Morale), in which he warned against the dangers of speculation and the decline of public morale in general.[1] The guilds will lay down statutes for all their members and establish Courts of Honour before which every member contravening these statutes will be brought.[2]

Just at the time when Gökalp published his final ideas on the value of such associations (1922–3), a corporative State appeared in Fascist Italy. Gökalp, however, with all his bias in favour of Society as against the individual, does not, as we have seen, want to establish a totalitarian State. He explicitly demands that the guilds should remain independent and that the State should not interfere in their activities.[3]

These ideas about the importance and the functions of the guilds are taken from Durkheim.[4] The theories of the French sociologist were based on the experience of a country in which the Trade Union movement was well developed. However, in Turkey not even the foundations of such organizations had been

---

[1] Fahri, p. 101, *n.* 2.
[2] K.E., pp. 122–3; Y.M., 32, p. 104b; 35, p. 162b; K.M., 11; E., pp. 80–81, 142–4.
[3] E., p. 162.
[4] See *Division*, préface; *Suicide*, pp. 435–50.

9

laid and the people were hardly capable of establishing independent guilds of this kind. This is one of the many cases in which Gökalp accepted from the West theories which did not entirely suit the conditions of his own country.

### POLITICAL ECONOMY

From the *Tanzimat* period onwards the economic condition of Turkey suffered a rapid decline. With the gradual Westernization of Turkish life the traditional crafts were ruined, and economic key positions passed into the hands of foreigners and of members of the non-Muslim communities that had already previously played a considerable part in commerce and industry. Incidentally, Gökalp maintains, this economic decline and the lack of a Turkish middle class affected also cultural life adversely. The Turkish intellectuals were mostly officials with a low salary and without sufficient spare time to devote to studies and creative work.[1]

For the development of a modern economy Gökalp seeks first of all to remove the harmful legacy of Islamic traditions, such as the pious foundations, the tithe, and the prohibition of interest. While in the beginning he favours a capitalistic régime and demands the creation of a strong Muslim Turkish middle class, he later turns against the theories of Manchester liberalism which were current in Turkey from the time of the *Tanzimat*. Opposing all State intervention in economic life, these theories are not suited to conditions in Turkey which, unlike England, is a backward agricultural country without any considerable export. By adopting the principle of Free Trade the Ottoman Empire condemned itself to economic servitude to the great industrial countries. If Turkey wants to modernize its economic life and in particular to develop its industries, she must adopt a system of national economy as outlined by the American John Rae and the German Friedrich

[1] T., pp. 5–6; K.M., 23; E., p. 56.

List.[1] A first step in this direction is the backing of local industries against foreign competition. In his poem "Economic Patriotism" [2] and other writings Gökalp calls on the public to buy local products (*yerli mal*) instead of the "rotten" goods imported from Europe.

Gökalp's later writings on this subject advocate a radical change in the attitude of the Young Turks, who in the beginning of their rule had remained loyal to the principles of Free Trade and of preference to agriculture over industry. To counter the influence of the *Ulum-ü İçtimaiye ve İktisadiye Mecmuası* (Review of Sociology and Economics), which served in those days as the organ of liberal economists, Gökalp took an active part in the establishment of the *İktisat Derneği* (Economic Association) and the publication of the *İktisadiyat Mecmuası* (Economic Review) which propagated the idea of State intervention in economic affairs. [3]

The effects of the First World War on Turkish economic life made the leaders of Union and Progress more disposed to accept Gökalp's views. The abolition of the Capitulations in the beginning of the war enabled the Government to follow an active tariff policy for the protection of national industry. Further steps in national economic planning were the establishment of the *İtibar-ı Millî Bankası* (National Credit Bank), the preparations for building a railway line to Ankara by the State, and particularly the issuing of a national loan.[4] Gökalp, however, goes further and demands the establishment of a Ministry of National Economy which shall direct economic life, control customs, railways, ports and the National Bank, and draft social legislation. He maintains that private enterprise in Turkey is too weak to carry out a comprehensive programme of economic development. For this reason and

[1] As one of the fathers of Pan-Germanism List seems to have particularly attracted Gökalp's attention.

[2] *İktisadî Vatanperverlik* (K.M., 1); see also K.E., pp. 120–21.

[3] Fındıkoğlu, op. cit., pp. 54 *sq.*

[4] Another measure, which Gökalp does not mention, was the 1916 law compelling all companies to use the Turkish language in their business transactions (see Ahmed Emin, p. 114).

because of the lack of trained technicians the Government, the provinces, and the municipalities must take the initiative and start industrial undertakings with the help of foreign experts. The workshops which Atatürk's Army established during the Anatolian war could serve as a model.[1]

Gökalp's ideas pointed the way to the peculiar form of State capitalism that developed in Kemalist Turkey. After the economic world crisis in 1929 Atatürk's Government embarked on an energetic policy of State enterprise, which found its most striking expression in the Five Years Plans for the development of industries, communications and other economic resources of the country. The principle of *étatisme* (*devletçilik*) is said to have received official recognition for the first time in 1930 in a speech made by İsmet İnönü on the occasion of the opening of the railway line to Sevas.[2] It was subsequently incorporated into the programme of the Government party (the Republican People's Party) and later laid down in the Constitution of the Republic as one of the fundamental principles of the new Turkish State.

[1] Y.M., 43, pp. 322c–323a; Y.H., p. 9; K.M., 23; E., pp. 69, 168–9; see also *İktisadiyat Mecmuası*, 1917.
[2] Ahmet Hamdi Başar, *Dâvalarımız* (Istanbul, 1943), p. 29.

# VI

# "TURKIFICATION, ISLAMIZATION, MODERNIZATION"

In his well-known article published in 1904 Akçoraoğlu [1] discusses the merits and demerits of "Three Ways of Policy"— Ottomanism, Pan-Islamism and Turanism. Gökalp does not accept any of these Ways, but tries to combine certain basic ideas of each in his conception of Turkism. In 1918 he published in book form a collection of his articles which had appeared in 1913–14 in *Türk Yurdu* under the title *Türkleşmek, İslâmlaşmak, Muasırlaşmak* (Turkification, Islamization, Modernization). [2] He borrowed these watchwords from the writings of his friend Hüseyinzade Ali, who as early as 1907 had in his Baku periodical *Füyuzat* summoned the Turks to *Türkleşmek, İslâmlaşmak, Avrupalılaşmak*. [3] By this motto Hüseyinzade meant "to be inspired by Turkish life, to worship God in accordance with the Muslim religion and to adopt present-day European civilization." [4]

Gökalp made this principle the foundation of his teachings and elaborated it both theoretically and practically. His slogan was: "We belong to the Turkish nation, the Muslim religious community and the European civilization." Unlike Akçoraoğlu, however, he refuses to base his demand for modernization on the liberalism of the Ottomanist reformers, since political development had rendered such a course wholly impracticable. For the same reason and because of his conviction that political unity must be

---

[1] Akçoraoglu Yusuf, *Üç Tarz-ı Siyaset*, pp. 3–32.

[2] See p. 34, *n.* 2, *ante*.

[3] İsmail Habib Sevük, *Edebî Yeniliğimiz* (Istanbul, 1939), p. 412. See also Akçoraoğlu's account in his article *Gök Alp Ziya Bey* quoted in Şapolyo (p. 99).

[4] M. Hartmann, XX, p. 134, *n.* 2. According to Akçoraoğlu (*Türk Yılı*, 1928, p. 417) this motto had already been outlined by Hüseyinzade in the Baku paper *Hayat* in 1905.

preceded by cultural homogeneity he rejects, at least for the time being and as a practical programme, Pan-Islamism and Pan-Turkism or Turanism. From the first of these movements he accepts the element of Islam as one of the foundations of Turkish culture, while with regard to the second he limits the ideal of nationalism to the modern Turkish State only, seeking to maintain merely cultural relations with Muslims and Turks outside its borders.

Akçoraoğlu admitted that his "Three Ways" were to some extent contradictory.[1] Gökalp, on the other hand, claims that the basic elements of his ideology are not only compatible with each other but even mutually complementary. He bases this assumption on his distinction between national culture (*hars*), community of religion (*ümmet*) and international civilization (*medeniyet*). To each of these elements he allots its special place in the combination of the factors which are to determine the spiritual structure of modern Turkey. In his opinion the Turks should accept from Western civilization only the *maddiyat*, its material achievements and scientific methods, and from Islam its religious beliefs without its political, legal and social traditions. All the other elements of culture, and particularly all the emotional and moral values (*maneviyat*), except the religious ones, should be drawn from Turkish heritage. A typical example of his application of this theory is the treatment of language as described above.[2]

This rigid and artificial distinction did not prove workable, since it lacked consistency and did not correspond to the reality of modern Turkish life. In Gökalp's synthesis of Turkish culture and Western civilization there is no proper place for Islam as a third element. As far as Islam belongs to the sphere of civilization, it has to be superseded by modern European values. Most of its "cultural" elements should, if Gökalp were consistent, be regarded as part of Arab or Persian national culture, which should not be accepted by the Turks. Although Gökalp is at a loss to find

[1] Akçoraoğlu, op cit., pp. 15–16.    [2] P. 119.

the roots of Islam in Turkish national traditions, he does not suggest the development of a specifically Turkish Islam. His "religious Turkism"[1] is one of the weakest points in his programme for the cultural revival of his nation, consisting merely of the demand to introduce the Turkish language into the religious service. It is significant that Gökalp never tries to expound his conception of Islam as a purely ethical religion. For him it is only important to state what Islam does *not* imply any more, and what has to be eliminated because of its incompatibility with the major factors of Turkish culture and Western civilization. As rightly observed by Bergsträsser,[2] Gökalp's system does not allow religion any separate existence. The definition of *İslâm ümmetçiliği*, the Islamic element in Turkish life, as an independent factor of major importance was from the beginning vague and unconvincing and was necessitated mainly by the structure of the Ottoman Empire. With the dissolution of this empire, Islam gradually lost its value in Gökalp's teachings and became the junior partner in his trinity.

In the development of the Turkish Republic after Gökalp's death the religious element has been eliminated and Westernization has exercised a growing influence, performing a considerable part of the functions which Gökalp had allotted to the Turkish national culture. The foundations of Kemalism are *Türkçülük* and *Garpçılık* (Turkism and Westernism) only. While the former was insistently declared to be the most important element, the latter has in fact become the paramount influence in many spheres of modern Turkish culture.

[1] E., pp. 163–4.
[2] G. Bergsträsser, *Islam und Abendland*, p. 25.

# PART THREE

# APPRECIATION
# OF ZİYA GÖKALP

# I

# ZİYA GÖKALP, THE SCHOLAR AND POET

In one of his theoretical articles [1] Gökalp lays down that all scientific research should be conducted objectively, *sine ira et studio* and without any ulterior motive. In general, however, he is far from living up to his own principle. In his writings a subjective approach, favourable or unfavourable to his subject, is only too manifest. His definitions of many basic terms, such as *hars* (culture), *medeniyet* (civilization), *kozmopolitizm* and others, betray an emotional bias. Furthermore, he often changes his views even on major problems to suit political circumstances. His attitude to Turanism, to the status of the Arabs in the Ottoman Empire, and especially to the question of the Sultanate are typical examples. Many of the subjects he deals with are so closely interwoven with current affairs that, even if he had desired, he could not always have avoided overstepping the line which divides the work of the scholar from that of the politician and publicist. In fact he is deeply interested in both fields, sociological research and the practical application of his theories.

While Durkheim, too, hoped that his works would influence social and political action, he was first of all a scholar, whose main object was to establish scientific truth. Gökalp is less cautious and detached, tending to evaluate phenomena where the French sociologist merely tries to state and explain facts. Gökalp likes to give his ideas the form of a "dogma" which the leaders of public life ought to follow. In doing so he reveals what Ülken [2] fittingly calls the "old mentality of a Mufti in European dress". The categorical

[1] M.T.M., 2, pp. 193–6.
[2] Ülken, p. 37.

155

rules in Gökalp's catechism are based not on the law of Islam but
on Durkheim's sociology.

Gökalp does not always apply the inductive method which in
his opinion [1] is the only correct way to investigate sociological
questions. Unlike Western sociologists, he often bases his views
not on historical, economic or statistical facts (little preparatory research work of this kind had been done in the Turkey of
his days),[2] but on inferences and deductions which sometimes
become a mere play on words. Characteristic is his fondness for
analysing and expounding sociological problems by definition of
terms and particularly of two contrasting terms, such as individual
and society, culture and civilization, class and guild.[3] In many
instances he thinks that he has found the solution to a practical
problem if he has succeeded in devising a suitable formula. He
often gives the impression of first working out a theory and then
looking for proofs or illustrations to support it. The result is that
he ignores many facts which do not fit in with his theories and
distorts others to make them suit his requirements. Even his
friends and colleagues criticized his excessive liking for theoretical
and abstract thinking. It is true that his insistence on defining
scientific terms has helped to train his contemporaries in more
precise habits of thought. But as a result of the development of
the Turkish language after his death the majority of his terms,
mostly formed from Arabic words, were replaced by others
taken from European languages or newly created from Turkish
roots.

Gökalp's scholastic leanings are also shown by his habit of
quoting the Qur'ān and Ḥadīth in support of his ideas, although in
theory he strongly objects to this method. There is often the same
"obvious strain between the plain sense and religious purport of

[1] M.T.M., loc. cit.

[2] Prior to 1927, for instance, no modern census had been taken in Turkey
(Ahmed Emin, p. xi).

[3] Durkheim too assigned an all-important function to definitions (see
H. Alpert, *E. Durkheim and His Sociology*, pp. 114–19).

the verse and the doctrine to which (he) has fitted it" which has been observed in the writings of the Indian reformer Sir Muḥam-mad Iqbāl.[1] It is difficult to decide whether Gökalp adopts this practice, as Ziyaeddin Fahri [2] thinks, because he believes in the principles of Islam or solely for tactical reasons.

Another contradiction between theory and practice appears in Gökalp's protests against the dilettantism of the *Tanzimat* writers, who dealt with all kinds of questions without possessing a thorough knowledge of any field. Gökalp is hardly the right person to criticize dilettantism. He himself does not hesitate to deal with many different subjects, politics and law, sociology and economics, religion and philology, without a proper scientific equipment in most of them. It is obvious from his writings that he was self-educated and that he had never visited Europe. Despite all his efforts his Western education remained fragmentary. Except for French he did not know any European language, and his know-ledge of German philosophy and sociology is taken from secondary sources.

With all these deficiencies there is no doubt that his efforts to establish scientific research on European lines had a beneficial influence on the Turkish intelligentsia. In particular he played an important part by being the first Turk who used the methods of modern sociology for a systematic research into Turkish history, civilization and social conditions. Among Gökalp's disciples there are a number of well-known Turkish sociologists, such as İsmail Hakkı Baltacıoğlu, Mehmet Servet, Mehmet İzzet, Ziyaeddin Fahri and others. Köprülüzade (Fuat Köprülü), another of his disciples, successfully introduced sociological methods into the study of Turkish literary history.[3] Halide Edib and Tekin Alp, who both acknowledged Gökalp as their teacher, made use of his

---

[1] H. A. R. Gibb, op. cit., p. 83.

[2] P. 192.

[3] See his books *Türk Edebiyatında Ilk Mütesavvıflar*, 1919, and *Türk Edebiyatı Tarihi*, 1920–21; and his article *Türk Edebiyatı Tarihinde Usul* in M.T.M., 1.

ideas in their attempts to explain modern Turkey to the West.[1] Ardent believers in Kemalist *étatisme*, such as Ahmet Hamdi Başar, criticize Gökalp for having—at least in his early writings— supported a liberal and capitalistic régime, but accept his teachings in principle and call him "the only one of our scholars and thinkers who has studied our conditions by European methods".[2] Peyami Safa[3] and other advocates of complete Westernization, while criticizing Gökalp's hesitations in his fight against Islamic traditions and institutions, also base their views largely on his writings.

Gökalp's new approach to Islam and its history is particularly noteworthy,[4] and it is unfortunate that the political development in Turkey has discouraged Turkish scholars from continuing his studies. Although his ideas on the reform of Islamic law have no more than an academic interest in modern Turkey, which has become an entirely secular State, they may be of practical importance for the rest of the Muslim world. His basic theory of the *örf*, the social element, as the major factor in canon law seems, however, not to have been accepted by any Arab modernist.[5]

Although he published many books and articles on Turkish history, Gökalp was far from being a historian in the Western sense. He regarded history mainly as ancillary to sociology and as a kind of storehouse of facts to illustrate his sociological theories. Political history did not interest him at all, and he explicitly gave it as his opinion that "history should in general be the history of civilization".[6] Though he tried to explain to his contemporaries the methods of modern European historiography with its criticism, objectivity and classification of sources,[7] he

---

[1] Halide Edib, *Turkey Faces West*, 1930; Tekin Alp, *Le Kemalisme*, 1937.

[2] A. Hamdi Başar, *Dâvalarımız* (Istanbul, 1943), p. 37.

[3] *Türk İnkılâbına Bakışlar*, Istanbul, 1938.

[4] Cf. M. Horten's view: "Die Philosophie von Ziya Gök Alp ist berufen, in wichtigen Punkten an einer Neugestaltung des Islam mitzuwirken" (*Der Islam*, VIII, p. 339).

[5] See H. A. R. Gibb, op. cit., p. 92.

[6] K.M., 17.

[7] Mainly in K.M., 11–16.

himself did not always live up to these standards. For instance, he often erred and misled others by trying at all costs to find analogies between the history of Turkish and Muslim culture and developments in Europe. His attempts to transfer terms of Western history, such as Renaissance, Reformation and Romanticism to the culture of the East [1] were risky and likely to give a wrong idea both of the terms and of the facts.

Gökalp's main interest lay not in "objective history", but in what he called "national history", and this he regarded as an art (*sanat*) rather than a science.[2] Like the German historian Treitschke, whom he quoted, he wanted to know the past, in order to create the future. The principal task of historical research for Gökalp was pedagogic—to strengthen Turkish patriotism by describing the brilliant past of his nation.[3] With this aim in view he wrote numerous articles on the history of the ancient Turks. This part of Gökalp's work has not been dealt with in this study it may be sufficient to point out that he lacked the necessary grounding, both historical and philological, for original research work in this field. He took his information mainly from secondary and tertiary sources, and often from sources of doubtful value. His writings on these subjects added little to Turcological knowledge, and many of his conclusions are at variance with the results of modern scholarship.

However, here too Gökalp's importance lay in the fact that he aroused the interest of the Turkish intellectuals in the ancient, particularly pre-Islamic, history of their nation. Since his death Turcology in Turkish universities, has made considerable progress due at least partly to Gökalp's pioneer work. Especially popular has become his thesis of the three stages of Ottoman-Turkish history. In the first the Turks were a racial group (*kavım*) in Central Asia, in the second a religious community (*ümmet*) in the

---

[1] See, for instance, his article *Tevfik Fikret ve Rönesans* in *Muallim Mecmuası* (II, 14).

[2] Cf. Durkheim's similar views on history, and especially the teaching of history, in *Educ. morale*, pp. 315 *sq.*    [3] K.M., 11.

Ottoman Empire, and in the third a modern nation (*millet*) inside the borders of the new Turkey. Turkish culture merged successively with three foreign civilizations (Chinese, Arab-Persian, European) and adjusted itself to three different "religions" (Shamanism, Islam, modern science).

In the field of Turkish folklore too Gökalp laid the foundation for future research. Keenly interested as he was in the culture of the common people (*halk*), he attached great importance to all forms of folklore—fairy tales, popular songs, proverbs, and religious beliefs which were still living among the Turkish people and many of which had originated in pre-Islamic times. Gökalp himself did some research work on folklore, for which he used the Turkish term *halkıyat*. Just as in eighteenth-century Germany Klopstock replaced Christian and Greco-Roman mythology with German and Nordic myths, so Gökalp published old Turkish legends and stories and searched for information on different aspects of popular culture. He also urged his young students to collect such material systematically.[1] Under his influence the study of popular literature was continued by Fuat Köprülü, Saadettin Nüzhet and others. The People's Houses (*Halkevleri*), the successors of the *Türk Ocağı*, which to-day exist in every Turkish town, have made it one of their chief tasks to study local folklore.

Gökalp the scholar often clashed with Gökalp the poet. This contradiction found a striking expression in his famous poem *Turan*. Gökalp refuses to accept the description of Attila and Jenghiz Khan as he found them in the historical sources. Accusing historiography of deliberately defaming these Turkish national heroes, he evokes their memories as well as that of Oğuz Han, the legendary ancestor of the Turks, from his feelings.

> Oğuz Han, whose figure remained vague to the scholar,
> Is clearly and fully known to my heart.
> In my blood he lives in all his fame and splendour.[2]

[1] K.M., 14; 18; 23; E., pp. 83–5.      [2] K.E., p. 13.

Like all romanticists Gökalp attaches special importance to feelings, instinct, the unconscious and subconscious. He quotes modern psychologists to prove that emotions are the basis for the intellectual activities of man.[1] "Don't think without feeling, . . . your emotion shall guide your mind."[2] Gökalp's opponents accuse him—as Durkheim was accused before—of harbouring some hidden mystical tendency. Şadan, for instance, obviously refers to Gökalp when he attacks the "University teachers who under Durkheim's colours concealed the mysticism of the *Divan* literature."[3]

While generally adapting Durkheim's theories to his purposes and beliefs Gökalp goes much farther than his teacher in attributing to society, which for him is identical with the nation, a "personality" or spiritual existence amounting almost to a metaphysical substance. His belief in the national soul or spirit (*ruh*), which he calls the "metahistorical" force (*mabadüttarih*) in the development of the Turkish nation,[4] often clashes with his endeavour to find scientific, that is rationalistic, proofs for his theories. Thus he often uses the results of his research in ancient Turkish history or Turkish folklore and ethnography to justify the acceptance of modern and Western ideals, such as democracy, monogamy, etc. While these ideals were actually the fruit of recent social and political development in his country, he tries to find their roots in the past, the national traditions and characteristics of the Turks. It is typical that he sometimes rejects a theory[5] because it does not conform to the national spirit, while later on he gives the more realistic reason that it does not suit the economic and social conditions of contemporary Turkey.

This fundamental contrast in Gökalp's mind between romanticism and realism, between an idealistic and a practical outlook is

[1] K.M., 28.
[2] K.E., p. 85.
[3] Dr. İzzeddin Şadan, *Birsam-ı Saadet* (Istanbul, 1943), p. 29.
[4] T., p. 17.
[5] Such as the economic theory of *laissez faire* in K.M., 23.

clearly reflected in his poem *Kızıl Elma*. Here dreams and visions merge with discussion of the practical problems of his day, and fantastic allegory is strangely mixed with prosaic matter-of-fact description. In recent years Gökalp's idealism (*mefkûrecilik*) has been strongly criticized by many Turkish writers [1] who represent the more realistic approach of the Kemalist revolution.

Gökalp regarded himself as a philosopher and a poet.[2] The former term, however, is for him identical with thinker in a general sense. He was little interested in systematic philosophy and particularly disliked metaphysics. Regarding his second claim, he can, from a purely aesthetic point of view, hardly be considered as a poet of rank. With all his ability to express his thoughts clearly and precisely in verse, his poems lack grace of form and beauty of language. Even his famous poem *Turan* was criticized by his contemporaries for this reason.[3] Moreover, very few of his poems show real poetic inspiration. The reader always feels that Gökalp is chiefly concerned with the thought he wishes to express. Gökalp knew his own shortcomings well enough. In the preface to his anthology *Yeni Hayat* he remarks in his usual sweeping way that his time is a "period of consciousness" in which the Muses are silent. Metre and rhyme have become the tools of versifiers (*müteşairler*) who are impelled to write not by poetic inspiration but by their conscious mind. "For the sake of the education of the people," however, it is fitting and useful to clothe certain ideas in verse form.

This urge to teach and educate was one of Gökalp's principal characteristics. In this occupation all his different and often contradictory impulses found scope. His friend Akçoraoğlu [4] rightly points out that Gökalp resembles those romantic German philosophers of the early nineteenth century like Fichte whose main

[1] Such as Peyami Safa, Hilmi Ziya Ülken and others. Cf. also Necati Akder's article (see Bibliography).

[2] See his letters from Malta (Ali Nüzhet, p. 103).

[3] See Ali Canip's criticism as quoted in the preface to *Altın Işık*, p. 5.

[4] In his article *Gök Alp Ziya Bey*, published in *Türk Yurdu* (see Şapolyo, p. 99).

object was to educate the masses and to work for the national revival both in theory and practice. Even more striking is Gökalp's similarity to another German thinker, H. von Treitschke, who like him was a university professor, journalist and Member of Parliament, and who also had a tremendous influence on the youth. "Treitschke is not an original thinker who, in the seclusion of his study, has elaborated his own system of thought. He is an eminently representative personality, and it is in this respect that he is instructive. Deeply involved in the life of his time, he expresses the mentality of his *milieu*." This appreciation of Treitschke by Durkheim [1] seems entirely applicable to Gökalp.

[1] *L'Allemagne*, p. 5.

# II

# ZİYA GÖKALP'S NATIONALISM

Political Science tends to distinguish between two main forms of nationalism.[1] In Western Europe, particularly in England and France, the united national State preceded the emergence of the nation and to a large extent even created it. When in the eighteenth century modern nationalism developed in these countries, it was based on the contemporary philosophy of Enlightenment with its rational approach and its individualist and universalist outlook. Most Western European writers of that period stressed the Natural Rights of man, the limits of governmental authority and the similarities between all human beings. Political thought in England and France has "on the whole emphasized the political and subjective aspect (of nationalism), connecting the nation closely with the State and finding the test of nationality in personal feeling."

In Germany and other Central and Eastern European countries, on the other hand, nationalism took a different form. The development of a strong German nationalism in the nineteenth century—several generations after its emergence in the West—preceded the birth of a united German State, the creation of which it regarded as its main object. German nationalism was largely the child of romanticism which attached major importance to emotions and stressed the natural peculiarities of the different nations. Regarding the nation primarily as a cultural and racial entity, it tried to find objective marks of nationality such as the *Volksgeist*, the spirit of the people, as expressed in its language and other cultural phenomena. German nationalism tended to be on the whole irrational, collectivistic, and exclusive.

[1] For the following, see Royal Institute of International Affairs, *Nationalism* (1939), pp. 31–5; H. Kohn, *The Idea of Nationalism* (New York, 1944), p. 574.

Although Gökalp borrowed most of his theories from French sociology and philosophy, his nationalism is more of the Central European and particularly German type. There is little evidence, however, of any direct influence of German thought on Gökalp. The German-Turkish rapprochement in the latter part of Abdul Hamid's rule and during the common fight in the First World War was limited mainly to political and military co-operation, although a number of German professors taught during the war at the Constantinople University. Even in this period the cultural influences to which the Turkish intelligentsia responded remained predominantly French. Very few German books were translated into Turkish. Gökalp did not know German, and the ideas of Herder and Fichte, Hegel and Nietzsche, Tönnies and Treitschke, which found an echo in his writings, reached him through French literature. Durkheim, who studied in Germany, and his collaborators had published reports and books on German sociology and philosophy. Gökalp is known to have perused *L'Année sociologique*, the important journal of social sciences which was edited by Durkheim and contained a large number of contributions by German scholars and reviews on German sociological works.

The main reason for the similarities between Gökalp's Turkism and German nationalism lies in the political and social conditions which in both countries differed from those in Western Europe. Autocratically ruled like Prussia, the Ottoman Empire assigned to the Army and bureaucracy a similar prominence. Officers and officials were the most respected citizens in both countries. Gökalp's demand for the complete subordination of the individual to society, though adopted from Durkheim, conforms to the Prussian ideal of absolute devotion of the citizen to the State even to the extinction of his personality. Gökalp discovered the supreme expression of the Turkish national character in the Army, which had just repulsed the Allied offensive at Gallipoli (1915), and hoped that Turkish art and science would in future be imbued with the same spirit.[1]

[1] Y.H., p. 19.

Like nationalism in most politically and socially backward countries Gökalp's Turkism found its first and main expression in the field of culture. "It was at the beginning the dream and hope of scholars and poets, unsupported by public opinion—which did not exist, and which the scholars and poets tried to create—a venture in education and propaganda rather than in policy-shaping and government." [1] Gökalp's preoccupation with national folklore and sagas, ancient customs and popular traditions, bears a striking similarity to the romantic school of German nationalism and the ideologies influenced by it (Mazzini in Italy, the Slavophils in Russia, etc.). In his book on the foundations of Turkism Gökalp deals separately with its linguistic, aesthetic, ethical, legal, religious, economic and philosophical aspects. Thus Turkism resembles German nationalism which "more than elsewhere . . . aspired to be not merely a political programme, but a complete philosophy of life." [2]

As in Germany of the early nineteenth century no wealthy middle class, like that which played so prominent a part in building the Western European nations, had developed in Turkey. Gökalp and his friends can hardly be called representatives of a bourgeoisie in the Western sense. They were a small group of intellectuals, journalists, writers and civil servants who had been influenced in various degrees by European thought. Opposed to the Court and the clergy—an aristocracy and a Church on the Western pattern never existed in Turkey—they regarded themselves as the future leaders of the national State. In the pursuit of their aims they joined forces with the most powerful element in the Ottoman State —the Army. To these professional, bureaucratic and military classes, or more precisely to a small active and revolutionary minority in them, nationalism opened the way to political power, and in their fight against foreign enemies they succeeded in gaining the support of the Turkish masses.

[1] H. Kohn, op. cit., pp. 329–30.
[2] R.I.A., op. cit., p. 41.

Although Gökalp did not represent an important middle class, his teachings (at least until 1919) are typical of a rising bourgeois movement and in parts strongly resemble the ideas of early Indian Muslim reformers such as Sir Sayyid Ahmad Khan and his school.[1] His attacks on blind obedience to ancient religious authority (*taklid*) and his demand for the virtual abolition of Muslim canon law, his fervent call for freedom of thought and revision of values in all spheres of life, his fight against the autocratic régime of the Sultans and the reactionary influence of the Muslim clergy, his insistent plea for the integration of women into the social and economic fabric of his nation—all these ideas reflect fundamental social changes, either already existing or, more often, wished for, in the Ottoman Empire. Gökalp's violent criticism of the lethargy of the Turkish people and the traditional contempt of their upper classes for trade and industry is reminiscent of Protestant preaching at the beginning of the capitalist era in Europe. His attitude is clearly shown when, demanding the creation of a strong Turkish middle class, he asserts that only the industrialists, artisans, merchants and professional people are important factors in economic life. The peasants who "benefit from the creative force of nature", and the Government officials who have no connection whatsoever with production are not creative elements at all. Only a régime based on the middle class (from which the civil servants are excluded) is, in Gökalp's opinion, able to set up a strong and efficient Government.[2] These views, typical of Gökalp's early liberal period, show a striking similarity to those of the leaders of the French Revolution in 1789. The Abbé Sieyès, for instance, in his famous pamphlet *What is the Third Estate?* identified the nation with the middle class, and in particular with the intellectuals and the wealthier bourgeoisie, which should be the only ruling class in the country.

In true liberal fashion Gökalp first hopes to realize his reforms

---

[1] See W. C. Smith, *Modern Islām in India* (London, 1946).
[2] T., pp. 5–6.

not by revolutionary acts (as later carried out by Atatürk) but by gradual evolution (*tekâmül*). The main force to bring about the necessary changes is education of the masses, on which Gökalp's interest was focused all his life. The social problems of the lower classes, however, were of little concern to him. References to the Turkish villagers, who constituted the bulk of the population, and suggestions of reforms on their behalf are astonishingly rare in his works. He hardly shows the same warmth of feeling for the unhappy plight of the Turkish peasant and worker as is found in the poems of his contemporaries Mehmet Akif and Mehmet Emin. As a typical bourgeois reformer Gökalp strongly advocates progress up to a certain stage, namely, the elimination of the feudal and aristocratic classes and the rule of the nationalist bourgeoisie. Further development in the direction of the rise of the working class is not envisaged. A Labour movement may develop in Turkey in the remote future when an industrial proletariat has come into existence, but even then socialism will have to be subject to the dominant ideal of nationalism. Gökalp hopes that in "solidarism" he has found a solution which will prevent all class struggle, just as some Indian reformers regarded Islam as a *via media* between capitalism and socialism.[1]

While in Western Europe nationalism was the expression of new economic, social and political conditions, it spread to Turkey, as to so many other Oriental countries, before such changes had gone very far. This is one of the main reasons for Gökalp's gradual departure from his early liberal ideas. He began to envisage the future Government of his national State not as the servant of the people but as its instructor and leader whose task it was to bring about the necessary changes. These concepts are found not only in the nationalist thought of backward societies. Already "in the case of Comte the inborn mysticism of Saint Simon's school had definitely overthrown the democratic ideal in favour of a new autocracy of scientific leadership."[2] The idea of leadership

[1] W. C. Smith, op. cit., pp. 90–91, 148.     [2] *Enc. of Social Sciences*, I., p. 168.

exercised by an " élite " seemed to Gökalp eminently suitable to conditions in Turkey where Western democracy could not work. In practice, therefore, he agreed to, or at least connived at, the semi-dictatorial rule of his party (Union and Progress) and theoretically prepared the ground for the future authoritarian leader (Mustafa Kemal).

In his fight against the despotism of Abdul Hamid and the clericalism of the *ulema* he adopted the liberal maxim of the free and independent personality which revolts against outworn traditions. Later, however, his Islamic education and the lack of a progressive bourgeois class among his people made him embrace Durkheim's theory of the absolute dominance of society over the individual. Although Gökalp demanded the merging of the individual in the nation, which may be called "one of the central points of totalitarian philosophy",[1] he can hardly be regarded as an advocate of the totalitarian State as it developed in the twentieth century in several European countries. He did not want to overthrow a liberal democratic régime or to achieve a classless State by liquidating the working-class organizations. Such demands are feasible only in a capitalist society, but not in Turkey where neither middle class nor proletariat had yet come into existence. Gökalp even advocated a Parliamentary régime and objected to State intervention in many spheres, particularly in the cultural field and in the activities of the guilds.

The fact that Turkish nationalism developed in a period of fierce struggle for national existence explains why in Gökalp's teachings almost no place is found for the ideals of humanity and international co-operation which his Muslim-Indian contemporary Sir Muḥammad Iqbāl so strongly professed. The faith in the ultimate value of the individual and in the oneness of humanity, which may have some restraining influence on nationalism, does not exist in Gökalp's theories.

As in the case of national movements in many Central and

[1] R.I.I.A., op. cit., p. 210.

Eastern European as well as Asiatic countries, Gökalp's nationalism was at the same time dependent upon and opposed to influences from the West. "Not rooted in a political and social reality, (it) lacked self-assurance; its inferiority complex was often compensated by over-emphasis and over-confidence." [1] His writings clearly illustrate one of the major inner problems of modern Turkish nationalism: the question of how to regain national self-respect and self-confidence which had been so deeply shaken by the continuous decline of Ottoman power and prestige vis-à-vis the West.

Gökalp's teachings form an indispensable link between the ideology of the Young Turks, in whose movement he played an important rôle, and Atatürk's régime. In the course of his literary activities (1909–24) he gradually turned away from the principles of the 1908–9 revolution (constitutional monarchy, Ottomanism, reform of Islam, capitalism, liberal democracy, evolutionism) and led the way to Kemalism based on the six pillars of republicanism, nationalism, secularism, *étatisme*, popular democracy and revolutionism. Though not sharing Atatürk's extreme views on all matters, Gökalp can claim to have laid the theoretical foundations for the modern Turkish State.

[1] H. Kohn, op. cit., p. 330.

# BIBLIOGRAPHY

## I. ZİYA GÖKALP'S WRITINGS

The bulk of Gökalp's writings are articles and poems published in newspapers and periodicals. Many of them later appeared in book form or were embodied with some changes in his books. While no full bibliography of his writings has yet been drawn up, more or less complete lists were published by Enver Behnan Şapolyo (pp. 246–69) and by Cahit Orhan in *İş Mecmuası*, 39–40 (1944), pp. 29–45. But these bibliographies too are insufficient in various respects; they do not cover all the writings published in newspapers nor do they mention the dates of publication of the separate articles and poems.

In the following a short list of Gökalp's main writings is given.

### 1. BOOKS

KIZIL ELMA   Istanbul, 1330 (1914–15); 1941.

"The Red Apple"; a collection of poems, some of which were previously published in various periodicals such as *Genç Kalemler*, *Rumeli*, *Halka Doğru*.

TÜRKLEŞMEK, İSLÂMLAŞMAK, MUASIRLAŞMAK   Istanbul, 1918.

"Turkification, Islamization, Modernization"; articles, most of which had been published before in *Türk Yurdu* and *İslâm Mecmuası* in the years 1913–14.

YENİ HAYAT   Istanbul, 1918; 1941.

"New Life"; a collection of poems, several of which had appeared in *İslâm Mecmuası* and *Yeni Mecmua*. In one of the 1918 editions of this book several poems were censored by the Government.

ALTIN IŞIK   Istanbul, 1339 (1923); 1942.

"The Golden Light"; poems, legends and a historical play, mostly from *Küçük Mecmua* (1922).

TÜRKÇÜLÜĞÜN ESASLARI   Ankara, 1339 (1923); Istanbul, 1940.

"The Foundations of Turkism"; expounding the programme of the Turkist movement. Many of its chapters were taken, with some changes, from *Yeni Mecmua* (68–9, 83–4) and *Küçük Mecmua* (5, etc.).

TÜRK TÜRESİ   Istanbul, 1339 (1923).

"Turkish Law"; a study of the religion of the ancient Turks.

DOĞRU YOL   *Hakimiyet-i Milliye ve Umderlerin Tasnif, Tahlil ve Tefsiri*   Ankara, 1339 (1923).

"The Right Way"; an explanation of the election programme of Mustafa Kemal's party.

TÜRK MEDENİYETİ TARİHİ   (*I. kısım*: *İslâmiyetten evvel Türk Medeniyeti*)   Istanbul, 1341 (1925).

"History of Turkish Civilization" (First Part: Pre-Islamic Turkish Civilization); for secondary schools. Further volumes did not appear.

## 2. ARTICLES

The number of Gökalp's articles and poems published during 15 years in various periodicals and newspapers amounts to over three hundred. For a list, although incomplete, of these writings see the bibliographies mentioned above. The periodicals in which most of his writings were published are:

| | | |
|---|---|---|
| *Rumeli* | Salonika | 1911 |
| *Genç Kalemler* | ,, | 1911 |
| *Türk Yurdu* | Istanbul | 1912–14 |
| *Halka Doğru* | ,, | 1913–14 |
| *Türk Sözü* | ,, | 1914 |
| *İslâm Mecmuası* | ,, | 1914–15 |
| *Millî Tetebbüler Mecmuası* | ,, | 1915 |
| *İktisadiyat Mecmuası* | ,, | 1916–18 |
| *Muallim Mecmuası* | ,, | 1916–17 |
| *İçtimaiyat Mecmuası* | ,, | 1917 |
| *Yeni Mecmua* | ,, | 1917–18, 1923 |
| *Şair Mecmuası* | ,, | 1918–19 |
| *İlim, Fen, Felsefe Tetebbuatı Mecmuası* | Ankara | 1922 |
| *Küçük Mecmua* | Diyarbekir | 1922–3 |

A number of his articles appeared in the following newspapers:

*Peyman, Dicle, Şûra-ı Ümmet*—Diyarbekir.

*Turan, Akşam, Tanin, Cumhuriyet*—Istanbul.

*Yeni Gün, Yeni Türkiye, Hakimiyet-i Milliye*—Ankara.

### 3. UNIVERSITY LECTURES

İLM-İ İÇTİMA   Istanbul, 1915.

"General Sociology"; see Rossi, p. 575, and Cahit Orhan, p. 31.

İLM-İ İÇTİMA-İ DİNİ   Istanbul, 1915 (?)

"Sociology of Religion"; see Cahit Orhan, p. 31.

Many of these lectures were published as articles in various periodicals.

İLM-İ İÇTİMA-İ HUKUKÎ

"Sociology of Law," according to Şapolyo, pp. 247, 267, these lectures were never published, while Cahit Orhan, p. 31, mentions their publication in 1330.

AMELÎ İÇTİMAİYAT

"Practical Sociology" (these lectures were not published except for one of them, *Halk ve Güzideler*, which appeared in *Çınaraltı Mecmuası*, 57, and was reprinted in Şapolyo, pp. 119–23).

### 4. UNPUBLISHED WRITINGS

*Kadın Hukuku* (Law of Women) see Cahit Orhan, p. 35; *Diyarbekir Destanı* (Tale of Diyarbekir) ibid, p. 37; *Büyük Türk Medeniyeti Tarihi* (Complete History of Turkish Civilization) see Şapolyo, p. 248; *Türkolojiye Müstenit Sosyoloji* (Sociology Based on Turkology) ibid; *Sosyoloji ve Psikolojiye Müstenit Felsefe* (Philosophy Based on Sociology and Psychology), ibid.

In addition Gökalp is said to have published a number of anonymous booklets and pamphlets in which he expressed radical views regarding the need for social and political changes (see Ahmed Emin, p. 234, and *Enc. of Social Sciences*, IV, p. 688).

Gökalp's scattered writings have not yet been collected. Many of his important articles, particularly those published in periodicals and newspapers, are to-day unavailable. The original editions of his works, published in the Arabic script, are not accessible to the younger generation in Turkey. Those of his writings which have later appeared in Latin script are often shortened and contain many mistakes. Several times since Gökalp's death committees have been formed with the idea of publishing all his works, but these plans never materialized. A complete and scholarly edition of his writings is highly desirable.

## II. BOOKS AND ARTICLES ON ZİYA GÖKALP

Akçoraoğlu Yusuf: *Üç Tarz-i Siyaset*. Istanbul, 1327.

Necati Akder: *Ziya Gökalp, âlim ve idealist şahsiyeti*. Ankara Üniv. Dil ve Tarih-Coğrafya Fakültesi Dergisi, III (1945), s. 2, pp. 159–81.

G. Bergstr* asser: *Islam und Abendland, Vom ägyptischen und türkischen Modernismus*. Auslandsstudien, 4. Band, Der Vordere Orient, Königsberg, 1929.

J. Deny: *Ziya Goek Alp*. Revue du monde musulman, tome 61 (1925, 3$^e$ trimestre), pp. 1–41.

Ahmed Emin: *Turkey in the World War*. New Haven, 1930.

A. Ziyaeddin Fahri: *Ziya Gökalp, sa vie et sa sociologie* (*Essai sur l'influence de la sociologie française en Turquie*). Paris, etc., 1935.

A. Fischer: *Aus der religiösen Reformbewegung in der Türkei*. Leipzig, 1922.

Martin Hartmann: *Aus der neueren osmanischen Dichtung*. Mitteilungen des Seminars für Orient. Sprachen, Berlin, 2. Abt., Westasiat. Studien, XIX, 1916, pp. 124–79; XX, 1917, pp. 86–149; XXI, 1918, pp. 1–82.

Richard Hartmann: *Ziya Gök Alp's Grundlagen des türkischen Nationakismus*. Orient. Lit. Zeit., 28. Jahrg., Nr. 9/10 (Sept.–Oct. 1925), pp. 578–610.

Ahmed Muhiddin: *Die Kulturbewegung im modernen Türkentum*. Leipzig, 1921.

Ali Nüzhet: *Ziya Gök Alpın Hayatı ve Malta Mektupları*. Istanbul, 1931.

Erich Pritsch: *Dichtungen Ziya Gökalps*. Festschrift Fr. Giese, Leipzig, 1941, pp. 119–28.

Ettore Rossi: *Uno Scrittore Turco Contemporaneo: Ziyā Gök Alp*. Oriente Mod., IV, 1924, pp. 574–595.

Peyami Safa: *Türk İnkılâbına Bakışlar*. Istanbul, 1938.

Enver Behnan Şayolyo: *Ziya Gökalp, İttihat ve Terakki ve Meşrutiyet Tarihi*. Istanbul, 1943.

Tekin Alp (M. Cohen): *Le Kemalisme*. Paris, 1937.

*Türk Yılı* (1928): *Türklük Fikri, Türkçülük Cereyanı, Türk Ocakları* (by Akçoraoğlu Yusuf, pp. 289–455.

Hilmi Ziya Ülken: *Ziya Gökalp*. Istanbul, Kanaat Kitabevi.